# The Bruno-Scarfo Mafia Crime Family

## The Complete History of a Philadelphia Criminal Organization

Mafia Library

© **Copyright 2023 - All rights reserved.**

The content contained within this book may not be reproduced, duplicated, or transmitted without direct written permission from the author or the publisher.

Under no circumstances will any blame or legal responsibility be held against the publisher, or author, for any damages, reparation, or monetary loss due to the information contained within this book, either directly or indirectly.

Legal Notice:

This book is copyright protected. It is only for personal use. You cannot amend, distribute, sell, use, quote or paraphrase any part, or the content within this book, without the consent of the author or publisher.

Disclaimer Notice:

Please note the information contained within this document is for educational and entertainment purposes only. All effort has been executed to present accurate, up to date, reliable, complete information. No warranties of any kind are declared or implied. Readers acknowledge that the author is not engaged in the rendering of legal, financial, medical, or professional advice. The content within this book has been derived from various sources. Please consult a licensed professional before attempting any techniques outlined in this book.

By reading this document, the reader agrees that under no circumstances is the author responsible for any losses, direct or indirect, that are incurred as a result of the use of the information contained within this document, including, but not limited to, errors, omissions, or inaccuracies.

# Table of Contents

INTRODUCTION ................................................................................................ 1

**CHAPTER 1: EARLY HISTORY OF THE PHILLY MOB** ........................................ 3

    ORIGINS ............................................................................................................ 3
    SALVATORE SABELLA AND EARLY CRIMINAL UNDERTAKINGS ................................. 5
    THE FIRST PHILADELPHIA MAFIA WAR .............................................................. 8
    THE EXPANSION OF JOSEPH 'JOE BRUNO' DOVI ................................................ 10

**CHAPTER 2: POWERFUL CONNECTIONS: VITO GENOVESE AND THE FIVE FAMILIES OF NEW YORK** ............................................................................. 13

    VITO GENOVESE AND THE FIVE FAMILIES ......................................................... 13
    JOSEPH IDA ...................................................................................................... 15
    THE PHILLY MOB AND THE COMMISSION ......................................................... 17
    THE 1957 APALACHIN MEETING ...................................................................... 19

**CHAPTER 3: 'THE GENTLE DON': ANGELO BRUNO** ................................... 21

    THE BRUNO CRIME FAMILY ............................................................................. 21
    THE GAMBINO CONNECTION ........................................................................... 24
    PRESSURE BEGINS TO BUILD ........................................................................... 25
    BRUNO'S MURDER .......................................................................................... 26

**CHAPTER 4: A STRUGGLE FOR POWER: THE SECOND PHILADELPHIA MAFIA WAR** ............................................................................................................. 29

    POWER VACUUM ............................................................................................ 29
    NICODEMO SCARFO TAKES POWER .................................................................. 31
    SCARFO'S RESHUFFLE ..................................................................................... 32
    NO TRIBUTE .................................................................................................... 33

**CHAPTER 5: THE GAMBLER'S FALLACY: ATLANTIC CITY** ........................... 37

    CRIME AND ATLANTIC CITY ............................................................................. 37
    FALL, THEN RISE ............................................................................................. 40
    SCARFO'S STOMPING GROUND ........................................................................ 42

**CHAPTER 6: RUTHLESS AND PARANOID: NICODEMO 'LITTLE NICKY' SCARFO** .... 45

    THE MOB UNDER SCARFO ............................................................................... 45
    THE MIND OF A MAFIA BOSS .......................................................................... 47
    SCARFO'S DOWNFALL ..................................................................................... 50
    RULING BEHIND BARS ..................................................................................... 52

**CHAPTER 7: THE WAR TO END ALL WARS: JOHN STANFA AND THE THIRD PHILADELPHIA MAFIA WAR** .................................................................................. 55

    THE APPOINTMENT OF STANFA ................................................................ 55
    A DIVIDE IN THE FAMILY ........................................................................ 57
    BUGGED AND JAILED ............................................................................ 60
    'FRONT BOSS' NATALE .......................................................................... 62

**CHAPTER 8: THE POLITICS OF CRIME: RALPH NATALE AND JOSEPH MERLINO** .. 65

    THE PUPPET BOSS ................................................................................ 65
    MERLINO'S NOTORIETY ......................................................................... 67
    KING RAT ............................................................................................ 68

**CHAPTER 9: TO FLEE A SINKING SHIP: RATS** .................................................. 71

    FROM COP TO BOUNCER TO SOLDIER: RON PREVITE ................................. 71
    CHILDHOOD MOBSTER: PHIL 'CRAZY PHIL' LEONETTI ................................ 74
    HEADSHOT SURVIVOR: JOHN VEASEY .................................................... 76
    SCARFO'S HITMAN: NICHOLAS 'NICKY CROW' CARAMANDI ....................... 81

**CHAPTER 10: THE 'MODERN' PHILLY MOB: JOSEPH LIGAMBI AND THE RETURN OF MERLINO** ............................................................................................. 85

    JOSEPH LIGAMBI .................................................................................. 85
    A PERIOD OF STABILITY ........................................................................ 87
    MERLINO'S RETURN ............................................................................. 89
    THE PHILLY MOB TODAY ...................................................................... 92

**CONCLUSION** ............................................................................................. 95

**REFERENCES** ............................................................................................. 97

# Introduction

*Mafia is a process, not a thing. Mafia is a form of clan; cooperation to which its individual members pledge lifelong loyalty. Friendship, connections, family ties, trust, loyalty, obedience: this was the glue that held us together.* –Joseph Bonanno

Organized crime, or more specifically, the Mafia, is an entity that has permeated society, catching fascination on multiple levels. One is through popular fictionalized content, including Francis Ford Coppola's *The Godfather* trilogy of films and, more recently, HBO's television series *The Sopranos* and *Boardwalk Empire*. Their accounts of self-made gangsters rising through the ranks, gaining wealth and power, through usually illicit means, against the backdrop of 20th century America have captivated audiences from their initial release until the present day. The above quote from Joseph Bonanno, who was Boss of the Bonanno Crime Family from 1931 to 1968, provides another perspective: one of cooperation, loyalty, and family, where the core tenants of the organization as a tightly knit unit truly encapsulate what it is to be a mafia family (Margaritoff, 2022). These films and shows do, of course, explore the Mafia, the key players within, and the activities organized crime are involved with, and Bonanno's quote provides an insider's perspective on the importance of loyalty and family within the Mafia. That being said, it is important that we do not become disconnected from one critical fact: that organized crime is a very real entity that both had and continues to have a stranglehold of influence on the society that we live in. The true nature of organized crime is then perhaps better understood as not solely encompassed by its representation in either the media or the quote from Bonanno, but in both, and, in intertwining the two, we come to see a more focused and accurate picture of organized crime as a whole.

Out of the numerous mafia organizations that arose and operated from the early 20th century and onward, there is one that tore a swathe of power, influence, and opulence from its inception to the modern day: the Philadelphia Crime Organization. Known by many names and colloquially as the Philly Mob, this organization carved out its territory initially in Philadelphia, then quickly moved its operations into other states, such as New Jersey and beyond. The Philly Mob's history is rife with bloody internal conflicts, shifting power structures, and aggressive expansion, cementing the organization in the annals of organized crime history as well as creating a sphere of influence that, within their territories, can be felt even today. From its beginnings as separate Italian-American street gangs, through to the rise and fall of various Bosses like Angelo Bruno, Nicodemo Scarfo, and Ralph Natale, to its position as a credible power within modern-day society under Joseph Merlino, this book will take you on a journey through the history of the Philly Mob, the plethora of dealings and activities it associated itself with, and the trail of carnage it left in its wake.

It seems then appropriate to kickstart this exploration with a newspaper headline, published in 1995 by The New York Times, that provides a perfect example of the nature and influence of the Philly Mob, as well as the lengths it would go to showcase its power: "Brother of Mob Turncoat is Gunned Down" (Raab, 1995).

# Chapter 1:
# Early History of the Philly Mob

As with many powerful and intricate crime organizations, the Philly Mob did not spring into existence as developed and influential as it came to be later. The organization's inception is a widely contested discussion point, with historians and journalists finding various sources that suggest multiple beginnings of the organization that would come to be known as the Philly Mob. Here, we will explore these points, journeying through the exploits and eventual amalgamation of the plethora of street gangs in Philadelphia. It would be this amalgamation that would be the beginnings of the Philly Mob that we still feel the influence of in the modern day.

## Origins

Shrouded in mystery and conflicting reports, the inception of an organized criminal outfit, or a Mafia, in Philadelphia sprung from the gangs that already existed and operated throughout the United States at the tail end of the 19th century. A slew of Sicilian and Italian immigrants had begun to settle in the United States at this time, and it is purported that "Americans [first] became acquainted with the word, 'Mafia' when the major wave of immigration of Sicilians…had settled in New Orleans in the 1860s" (Morello, 1999, p. 7). This organized criminal activity, while seen to be happening in other areas of the United States, such as New Orleans, Chicago, and New York, cannot be accurately linked to Philadelphia and its surrounding areas at this time in history. It seems that, towards the end of the 19th century, Philadelphia as a city had only "a secondary role in organized crime" (Morello, 1999, p. 13), with Secret Service agents who were attempting to stamp out the criminal activity at the time, finding only vague links with persons or groups in Philadelphia when arresting more extensive criminal networks in places like New York City. As Celeste Morello writes, "Identifying the Mafia was a difficult obstacle to overcome. Evidently, there was no proof of a Mafia in Philadelphia at that time" (Morello, 1999, pp. 13-14).

Of course, due to the very nature of organized criminal activity, just the fact that there was no proof of Mafia activity in Philadelphia does not mean that it did not exist. There are sources that suggest that "Mafiosi and Black Hand extortionists existed in the Philadelphia area from about the turn of the 20th century, possibly earlier" (Hunt, 2023). To clarify, mafioso refers to an official member of either the Sicilian or Italian-American Mafia, as well as any other Italian criminal organization. Black Hand refers to a type of Italian extortion racket brought to the United States with the Sicilian and Italian immigrants, operations of which were firmly rooted in numerous major American cities at the beginning of the 20th century, such as New York City, Chicago, and indeed Philadelphia. It is important to note at this point that Black Hand activity in Philadelphia, and indeed in the United States as a whole, was not so much an organized institution of individuals who dealt in criminal activities but more, so a method of extortion used by Italian mobsters. That being said, it is clear that, by the beginning of the 20th century, Black Hand activity is documented to have been occurring in Philadelphia, "overshadow[ing] all other 'Italian' ethnic crime by its overt symbols - the inked handprint and letters sent with demands" (Morello, 1999, p. 19). Indeed, Nicola Gentile (a Sicilian mafioso during this early period) published memoirs claiming, "that he was inducted into a crime family in Philadelphia around 1907", although this information is "confined to a footnote" and Gentile mentioned "nothing else about the organization or the city" (Hunt, 2023). Within the various criminal organizations operating in Philadelphia at this time, there were "deep factional divisions" (Hunt, 2023). While all were predominantly of Italian heritage, criminal individuals tended to drift towards groups that shared their specific regional identities. These groups included the more traditional Mafia organization of the western Sicilians, along with street gangs made up of Calabrians and eastern Sicilians. This by no means indicates a structured criminal organization present in Philadelphia, however, with "a significant division between Sicilian and Calabrian factions [lingering] in the crime family" even after consolidation (Hunt, 2023).

From this, we can see that, at this time, the existence of a singular and independent Philadelphia crime family is difficult to pinpoint and cohesively prove beyond a shadow of a doubt. On the other hand, we can see that criminal activities were indeed occurring within the city of Philadelphia and its surrounding areas, some of which can be at least somewhat linked to operations run by more extensive crime networks in other American cities. It seems clear that while it is evident that "Philadelphia indeed was a Mafia site of activity" at this time, it is quite unclear as to whether this was an independent entity in and of itself or was "an appendage of a New York Family" (Morello, 1999, p. 26). Regardless of the vague and mysterious beginnings of what would come to be known as the Philly Mob, the turn of the 20th century would see the apparent spattering of street gangs and criminal rackets coalesce into an independent and cohesive criminal organization, an organization headed by one particular man: Salvatore Sabella.

## Salvatore Sabella and Early Criminal Undertakings

Salvatore Sabella began his life in 1891, born to parents John and Rosa in Castellammare del Golfo, Sicily. It is interesting to note that numerous individuals who went on to become organized crime leaders in the United States came from this Sicilian town, including Sabella, Joseph Bonnano, and Stefano Magaddino, with Morello (1999) describing the area as "the birthplace of the Mafia" (p.41). Throughout Sabella's formative years, there is one instance that sent the young Sicilian on a journey that found him heading a crime organization of his own and, quite ironically, may have indeed prepared him for this calling. At fourteen years of age, Sabella found himself working as an apprentice to a butcher (a career path he would return to after his retirement from the Philly Mob in 1931). The butcher young Sabella worked under tended towards violent outbursts, the brunt of which seemed to fall upon Sabella. One fateful day in 1905, having had enough of the butcher's abuse, Sabella retaliated, killing him. Years later, in 1908, Sabella was charged for the butcher's murder and subsequently arrested, spending his three-year prison sentence in Milan, Italy. During his incarceration, it is thought that Sabella joined the Sicilian Mafia, promptly leaving for the United States after his release. Arriving in Brooklyn, New York, in 1912, Sabella quickly joined in with organized criminal activities, training to one day take a leadership role within the organization. That role came when, in 1919, Sabella was sent to Philadelphia to create a Sicilian criminal organization to operate there. With that, Salvatore Sabella joined the various street gangs and criminal organizations that operated in Philadelphia, becoming the first recognizable Boss of the Philly Mob.

The term 'recognizable' to describe Sabella's rise to power is used very specifically here, as it is predominantly clear that there were other leaders prior to Sabella. These leaders did not use the familiar titles and ran criminal activities that were not as organized as they were to become when Sabella took over. However, criminal enterprise in Philadelphia still existed prior to Sabella's arrival, and that enterprise required some vestige of hierarchy to operate effectively. As one of Sabella's soldiers stated, "There were many Bosses here before Salvatore Sabella" (Morello, 1999, p. 39). In fact, "to further [confuse] matters for historians," some of these early Bosses seemingly used the title of *rappresentante*, indicated to be "a sort of liaison or family ambassador" (Hunt, 2023). This role of *rappresentante* can be seen as a progenitor of sorts to the more formal designation of Boss that would come to be used later, with the *rapprensentante* acting as "a single regional spokesman for a fragmented underworld with multiple Bosses" (Hunt, 2023). With this in mind, it was these pockets of criminal enterprises that Sabella had to work with when he arrived in Philadelphia. Sabella set the beginnings of the Philly Mob on busying themselves with various criminal activities.

He led them to begin bootlegging: the smuggling of alcoholic beverages forbidden by law. Practically all of Sabella's reign as Boss was during Prohibition-era America. They began using extortion: the usually violent practice of gaining benefit through coercion. This was accompanied by loansharking: the practice of offering unlawful loans with extremely high-interest rates and usually violent consequences for failure to pay. They also began running illegal gambling rings: casino gambling was not made legal in the wider United States until much later in the century. There were factions of the criminal underworld in Philadelphia that did not appreciate Sabella's hostile takeover of their turf, arguably the most notable of which were the Zanghi brothers.

The Zanghi brothers, Anthony 'Muskie' Zanghi and Joseph Zanghi ran a local gang that feuded with Sabella's Philly Mob. While not acting wholly separate from the Philly Mob, the Zanghi brothers were known to be rebellious, seemingly preferring their own control as opposed to operating under the jurisdiction of Sabella. Having caused Sabella much trouble and difficulty, including being a suspect in the attempted murder of top lieutenant and future Boss John Avena, Sabella, along with Avena and others, decided to "send a message loud and clear: the streets of South Philadelphia were theirs - and would remain theirs" (Finkel, 2014). The message would come in 1927 when a drive-by shooting orchestrated by Sabella killed Joseph Zanghi and injured Anthony Zanghi. This hit would have consequences for Sabella, as the surviving Zanghi brother "broke the [gangster] code of silence" (Finkel, 2014), going straight to the police. Though Sabella was ultimately acquitted, the investigation led investigators to find Sabella to have entered the United States without proper documentation, ending with Sabella being deported back to Sicily later that year, with Avena taking over as acting Boss in Sabella's absence. The later years of Sabella's reign over the Philly Mob primarily took place outside of Philadelphia. He returned to the United States in 1929 to participate in the New York Castellammarese War. The conflict ended in 1931 with a victory for Sabella's side, and he returned to Philadelphia to resume control of the Philly Mob. This return, however, was short-lived. In the same year, Sabella was arrested once again for assault and battery with a motor vehicle. Shortly after, Sabella retired from organized crime, passing the leadership of the Philly Mob over to acting Boss John Avena. The reasoning for Sabella's retirement was and has remained unknown, and he was reported to have lived his life as a butcher in Norristown, Pennsylvania, until his death from natural causes in 1962. With Sabella retired and a criminal organization to run, Avena took his place as the new Boss. However, he was not without his challengers.

## The First Philadelphia Mafia War

As we will see time and time again during this exploration, the rank of Boss is a position that, when left empty, creates a bloody and drawn-out power struggle that ends with one victor sitting atop the carnage. Being no exception to this rule, the space at the head of the Philly Mob left after Sabella's departure was fought over in a five-year conflict known as the First Philadelphia Mafia War, with new Boss and alleged designated choice of his predecessor John Avena and another of Sabella's top lieutenants during his reign, Joseph 'Joe Bruno' Dovi heading the warring factions. Both men hailed from the Sicilian eastern region of Messina, with Avena born in 1893 and Dovi four years earlier in 1889. Another similarity between the two mobsters was that the majority of individuals taken into the fold of the Philly Mob had Western Sicilian heritage, with other regions of Sicily "generally regarded as outside the Mafia tradition" (Hunt, 2023). The 'made men' of the Philly Mob (in other words, the official and fully initiated members of the Mafia) at this time, despite usually requiring the individual to be Italian or of Italian descent, tended to be of this specific and traditional heritage. Regardless of this tradition, however, the main players in the First Philadelphia Mafia War were Avena and Dovi, and an ensuing battle for power was about to begin.

Avena had been close with Sabella, having been indicted along with him and others in the drive-by shooting of the Zanghi brothers, and was purportedly Sabella's choice to succeed him as Boss. Known as '*Nasone*' in Italian, translated to English as 'Big Nose,' Avena had been a staple in the Philadelphia criminal underworld since his arrival in the city in 1908. According to Hunt, Avena "reportedly moved into organized crime first as a Black Hand extortionist and later as a bootlegger and gambling racketeer" (Hunt, 2023). With the aforementioned indictment along with Sabella in 1927, Avena's standing within the Philly Mob seems to have been both respected and influential. Dovi, on the other hand, is harder to place in correlation to his activities within the organization before his grab for power, with his role within the Philly Mob during this time being "unclear" (Hunt, 2021). Born Giuseppe Dovi, but known more by his nickname 'Joe Bruno,' Dovi arrived in the United States as a teenager and moved and began operating in Philadelphia after a short stint in western New York state. While the details of Dovi's activities at this time are hazy, he was *consigliere* to Sabella, and he likely commanded a certain amount of power and influence within the Philly Mob, hence his challenge to Avena for the title of Boss.

The five-year conflict of the First Philadelphia Mafia War was bookended by the activities of a gang of criminal brothers: the Lanzetta brothers. The six brothers (Leo, Pius, Ignatius, Hugo, Lucian, and Teofilo) operated in South Philadelphia, involving themselves in various criminal activities. Their operation brought them into conflict with the Philly Mob, a conflict that went back to the days of Sabella's reign as Boss. Sabella was suspected of having been involved in the murder of Leo Lanzetta in 1925, and this grudge lasted into the reign of Avena. While the civil war between Avena and Dovi raged from 1931 to 1936, the "rebellious faction" led by the Lanzetti brothers "arose in the Philadelphia area" (Hunt, 2021). Under Avena, the Philly Mob had created a partnership with the Jewish 69th Street Mob, cementing them as leaders in the illegal gambling enterprise of Philadelphia. This power move brought the Philly Mob into direct conflict with the Lanzetta brothers, who also had a significant stake in the illegal gambling trade, worsening the already bubbling feud and "may ultimately have cost Avena his life" (Hunt, 2023). In 1936, the third attempt on Avena's life was successful, as Avena was shot to death in a brutal drive-by shooting. The Lanzetta brothers were key suspects in the murder, which effectively ended the First Philadelphia Mafia War and left the position of Boss of the Philly Mob open for the taking, a position filled without hesitation by Dovi.

## The Expansion of Joseph 'Joe Bruno' Dovi

Dovi officially became the Boss of the Philly Mob in 1936, wasting no time in consolidating and expanding the Philly Mob's operations in Philadelphia and beyond. Dovi had good connections with other powerful and influential crime organizations within the United States, including the Chicago Outfit (run by the infamous gangster Al 'Scarface' Capone) and the Five Families of New York (a formation of five major organized crime families operating out of New York City). These connections, along with a more aggressive and expansionist ideology from Dovi, allowed the Philly Mob to spread its influence across the Greater Philadelphia Area, Atlantic City, and even into southern New Jersey. The Philly Mob's activities and enterprises remained largely similar under Dovi, with the majority of the organization's income being from selling narcotics, along with the more familiar loansharking, extortion, and illegal gambling. Additionally, Dovi's tenure as Boss saw the settling of the long feud with the Lanzetta brothers, further solidifying the Philly Mob's hold over Philadelphia. This expansion also had another, more organic effect. With the ever-growing expansion of the Philly Mob came the interest of and connection with even more crime organizations, specifically the Gambino and Genovese crime families. Members of the Five Families of New York, these connections continued to grow throughout, and indeed long after, Dovi's reign as Boss.

Dovi was different from his predecessors. While Salvatore Sabella and John Avena held a similar philosophy, one of being 'hands-on' so to speak, in the affairs of the organization, Dovi held a diametric view, preferring to "[keep] his distance from the Philadelphia underworld" (Hunt, 2023). He ruled over the Philly Mob from various locations, none of which were in Philadelphia. Firstly, he dealt with his responsibilities as Boss from his residence in Bucks County, which was around 40 miles northeast of the city. Then, he relocated to Trenton, which, while technically closer, is in New Jersey. Both Sabella and Avena had resided in the city of Philadelphia itself. While this geographical point is interesting to make, it seems to have had no negative effect on Dovi's ability to effectively lead the Philly Mob to further prosperity throughout the late 1930s and well into the 1940s. In 1946, Dovi died of natural causes in a New York hospital, again leaving the Philly Mob without a Boss. However, the landscape of organized crime in the United States was changing, with the eyes of powerful individuals falling on the Philly Mob and its growing influence. They saw an opportunity and were most definitely going to seize it.

Chapter 2:
# Powerful Connections: Vito Genovese and the Five Families of New York

As we have seen in the previous chapter, the importance of connection within the world of organized crime cannot be understated. Those one knows and has a strong relationship with can be invaluable allies, especially in a cutthroat world where one's standing can rise and fall as quickly as the breeze changes. That being said, the state of the Philly Mob during the lead-up and at the death of Joseph Dovi was one of opportunity and expansion, a spreading fire fueled by some of the most powerful and influential criminal entities operating in the United States at the time. The Five Families of New York, specifically the Genovese Family, and even more specifically Vito Genovese, were the powers-that-be that drove the Philly Mob further up the hierarchy of criminal organizations. Here, we will explore the broader context of the organized criminal entities that surrounded the Philly Mob, the Philly Mob's connection to said entities, and the power shift that occurred in the criminal underworld of the United States, with the Philly Mob as the focus, during the 1940s up to the late 1950s.

## Vito Genovese and the Five Families

To call Vito Genovese an important individual in the context of the Mafia and organized crime in the United States would only be scratching the surface. That being said, there is very little space here to truly delve into the intricacies of Genovese himself and the wider Genovese crime family, who were one of the major players in the Five Families of New

York. What is prevalent here is the connection that Genovese and his family had to the rising organization, the Philly Mob. After the Castellammarese War in 1931, the same conflict that former Philly Mob Boss Salvatore Sabella took part in, Genovese and Luciano were integral to reorganizing the crime syndicates of the United States, officializing the Five Families and creating the Commission. In 1956, Genovese went from underboss to Boss of what would later be named the Genovese crime family when an assassination attempt, concocted by Genovese, on previous Boss Frank Costello failed to kill him, but did succeed in "[pushing] Costello into retirement" (*Notable Names: Vito Genovese*, 2015). Now head of a powerful crime family and having seen the gains made by the Philly Mob started by Joseph Dovi, Genovese made moves to exert control over the burgeoning organization from Philadelphia. So exceptional was the influence Genovese had on the Philly Mob in fact that, as the Philly Mob's growth continued into southern New Jersey and Atlantic City, many viewed it as simply as a Genovese faction as opposed to an independent crime organization.

In the same vein as Genovese, the other crime families of New York also looked towards the Philly Mob with eyes full of opportunity, wanting a cut of their profitable activities. The Five Families of New York had been set up in the aftermath of the Castellammarese War and was composed of the most powerful organized crime syndicates operating in the United States. The families that comprise the group are now known as the Bonnano, Colombo, Genovese, Gambino, and Lucchese families. At the organization's inception, each family was intended to report to Salvatore Maranzano, the victor of the Castellammarese War, who gave himself the title of '*capo dei capi*' or 'boss of all bosses.' This self-given, and some would argue vain, title drew ire, however, and Marazano was assassinated, the role of 'boss of all bosses' being replaced by the Commission. As we can see from this brief explanation of the Five Families, the Philly Mob is not mentioned as part of the conglomerate, further reinforcing the idea that the Philly Mob was not regarded as a top power in the Mafia families at this time. As previously mentioned, the Genovese family had a large influence over the Philly Mob, as did connections grow with Carlo Gambino, a high-ranking member of the Gambino crime family and ally of future Philly Mob Boss Angelo Bruno. Suffice it to say that these connections with other crime families both helped and hindered the Philly Mob: helped by allowing the organization to grow its own power and influence across a large area of the United States and hindered by devaluing the Philly Mob's position as a wholly independent criminal organization, demoting it to simply another appendage of the monster that was the Five Families of New York.

## Joseph Ida

Giuseppe 'Joseph' Ida was born in Fiumara, Italy, in 1890. The year 1919 saw Ida come to the United States, settling in the south of Philadelphia, where it seems he quickly found himself enveloped in the criminal activities of the Philly Mob. Purportedly, "there was always something to say about Joe Ida that was disconcerting. He was around for a while and supposedly was involved in everything from interstate prostitution to killings to gambling and narcotics" (Morello, 2005, p.58). At some point, Ida was introduced to then Boss Salvatore Sabella, his underboss John Avena, and *consigliere* Joseph 'Joe Bruno' Dovi. While it is complete conjecture to suggest that Ida met all three at the same time, Ida seemingly had, in quick succession, met all three of his predecessors. In fact, in the aftermath of the 1927 drive-by shooting of the Zanghi brothers, he was charged along with Sabella and Avena for his participation in the crime, although none were ultimately convicted. When Dovi took over as Boss after Avena's murder, he chose Ida as his underboss. After Dovi's death in 1946, the newly formed Commission appointed Ida as his successor. From Dovi, Ida inherited a Philly Mob that was steadily growing its power while also dealing with the grasping hands of other larger criminal organizations.

Ida was the Philly Mob's first non-Silician Boss and, like his predecessor Dovi, "lived some distance from Philadelphia during his term as Boss," his residence being "considerably closer to New York City than to Philadelphia" (Hunt, 2023). Again, just like his predecessor, this fact did not hinder Ida's ability to grow the Philly Mob's power and influence as, under his watchful eye, "the crime family reportedly expanded" (Hunt, 2023). Ida drove out the Jewish mobsters operating in Philly Mob territory, effectively ending the presence of the Jewish Mob in Philadelphia and southern New Jersey. It was also under the reign of Ida that "illegal narcotics were tied publicly to the Philadelphia-South Jersey Family as never before" (Morello, 2005, p. 71). The trafficking of narcotics, while, of course, a very risky business, saw massive returns in profit for those that involved themselves and were successful. As the Philly Mob continued to grow in South Jersey and Atlantic City, along with this push in the sale of narcotics, Ida felt the invasive hands of the Genovese family, which had been ever-present, grip further around his organization. The Genovese family sought to influence the comings and goings of numerous families, and as previously covered in this chapter, the growth of the Philly Mob was of particular interest to underboss Vito Genovese. This influence would stay for the moment, but under Ida, the Philly Mob continued to make their mark on the criminal underworld, pushing ever closer to their standing as an independent power in their own right.

At this point, instead of discussing the end of Ida's reign as Boss (a part of the Philly Mob's history that is intrinsically linked to an event that will be discussed later in this chapter), let us discuss the individual that took power (albeit briefly) directly after, acting as the bridge between Ida's reign and the reign of Philly Mob heavyweight Angelo Bruno: Antonio Pollina. From Sicily, Pollina had been active in the Philly Mob since at least 1927, with arrests for murder, assault, and concealed weapons, and was yet another one of the Philly Mob members to be indicted for the drive-by shooting of the Zanghi brothers. In late 1958, Pollina was thrust into the position of Boss after Ida departed from the United States. While seemingly more than happy to take the position (being the leader of an organized crime family does have its perks, after all), "the year 1959 would be unforgettable for Antonio Domenico Pollina" (Morello, 2005, p. 78). Serving his tenure as Boss from within the city of Philadelphia, Pollina's "proximity to the Philly rackets did not help his popularity with the crime family membership," and the Commission began to notice "deep division in the organization" (Hunt, 2023). This lack of recognition (the Commission reportedly designated Pollina as 'interim Boss' until order could be restored to the family) was made worse by Pollina, who began plotting to murder Angelo Bruno, a well-respected Mafia member and Pollina's self-decided rival. Why Pollina decided this is unclear; however, Bruno later commented that "it was just a manifestation of jealousy on Pollina's part" (Morello, 2005, p. 78). Due to the respect Bruno commanded, as well as Pollina's own underboss revealing his murder plans, Pollino was stripped of his power and forced to step down. The Commission even authorized Bruno to murder Pollina, although this did not happen, with Pollina living out his life "as a dishonored Mafioso" until his death at 101 years of age in 1993. Leaving with the words of Pollina himself towards the end of his life, "God wants me to live so I can suffer" (Morello, 2005, p. 99).

## The Philly Mob and the Commission

As we have seen, the Commission sprung into existence at the outset of the Castellammarese War in 1931. Its creation was in aid of overseeing all Mafia activity in the United States, to create a third party to mediate and solve disputes between families, to unify the collection of crime families and networks operating in the same territories and protect the interests of all criminal organizations under one overarching jurisdiction. After the debacle that was Maranzano and his 'boss of all bosses' moniker, those in power felt that the Commission was a less provocative and more efficient way of presiding over the criminal families of the United States. At its inception, the Commission was composed of a ruling committee on which sat each Boss of the Five Families of New

York as well as the Bosses of the Chicago Outfit. The Commission's responsibilities manifested in many ways, such as "approving new members, controlling relations between [the Commission] and the Sicilian Mafia, [and] formally recognizing new bosses" (Petepiece, 2018, p. 18). While this all sounds quite formal, let us not forget that the Commission oversaw all Mafia enterprises in the United States. These responsibilities sometimes required a darker and more brutal nature, "taking steps to maintain order between families including the use of murder and creating an atmosphere of fear concerning the Commission to ensure obedience" (Petepiece, 2018, p. 18). The Commission was not without its downfalls, with plots by members to assassinate other members being rather commonplace (the most well-known of these instances being Joe Bonnano's failed coup in 1963) as well as constant police attention and scrutiny, eventually leading to the Mafia Commission Trial in 1985. These future events aside, the Commission was, at this time, the new power in the criminal underworld, a power that the various crime families had to work with in order to continue their enterprises.

This is the landscape that Ida's Philly Mob found itself rising through the ranks around the mid-to-late 1950s. As has been made clear by both the setup of the Commission and the actions and influences of the larger crime families whose Bosses were committee members of said Commission, the Philly Mob was not at the table, so to speak, when it came to holding any power or sway within the ruling organization. This fact, however, was very rapidly approaching a complete turnaround. After a 1956 Commission meeting, the Philly Mob, along with the Detroit Partnership led by Joseph Zerilli and the Buffalo crime family headed by Stefano Magaddino, were inducted into the Commission, their leaders being given places on the committee. For the Philly Mob, this move onto the Commission cemented its position as a functioning and influential criminal organization in and of itself, one that acted independently from any other. This was a pivotal moment in the history of the Philly Mob, a moment where it garnered its reputation as a genuine power in the criminal underworld, paving the way for a slew of infamous

Bosses that came in the preceding decades, as well as its familiar title of the Bruno-Scarfo Mafia crime family. This is, however, jumping the gun somewhat, as Ida still firmly held control over the Philly Mob in 1956. That is, of course, until this firm grip began to loosen, the catalyst of which was the events of the Apalachin Meeting in 1957.

## The 1957 Apalachin Meeting

The 1957 Apalachin Meeting was a summit meeting of the American Mafia hosted at the home of mobster Joseph 'Joe the Barber' Barbara in Apalachin, New York. On the agenda for the meeting were allegedly topics such as narcotics trafficking, gambling, loansharking, and the dividing up of recently murdered mobster Albert Anastasia's illegal enterprises amongst the other criminal networks. The meeting also served another purpose. It gave Vito Genovese, who had just taken control of the Genovese crime family (named the Luciano crime family before his takeover) from Frank Costello, a way to legitimize his power by calling on the leaders of all crime families and criminal networks operating at the time to attend. Barbara's house was chosen as the location for the meeting as it was "200 miles northwest of New York City and the prying eyes of police" (Dunn, 2021). Over 100 Mafioso are reported to have attended, all "[barreling] down the highways to rural New York in sleek, brand-new Cadillacs" (Dunn, 2021). This detail is imperative, as it was this that tipped off the authorities as to what was occurring. New York State police detective Ed Croswell "saw dozens of gleaming Cadillacs parked next to the only paved stretch of backroad leading to Barbara's house" and immediately "knew something was up" (Dunn, 2021). With roadblocks set up, the police quickly raided the meeting. In an attempt to flee, many gangsters fled into the surrounding woods of Barbara's estate, clad in expensive jewelry and suits. Purportedly, locals in the area stated that, even months after the event, "they were still picking hundred-dollar bills out of the leaves in the woods around the house" (Dunn, 2021). In total, the authorities arrested and indicted 62 criminal Bosses, although the charges brought before them did not stick. However, an important outcome of the raid on the Apalachin Meeting was the shedding of light on the criminal underworld, an entity the existence of which authorities had long refused to acknowledge.

Coming back into relation with the Philly Mob, we can now pick back up with Joseph Ida, who, along with his underboss Dominick 'Big Dom' Oliveto, were of the many mobsters that attended the Apalachin Meeting and also were arrested when it was raided by law enforcement, Ida himself being identified and indicted on a drug trafficking charge. As Morello (2005) puts it, "Apalachin was Ida's downfall, a lasting defeat, a betrayal by so-called friends in a fellowship that he thought was more than a family" (pp. 73-74). Ida was taking no chances, fleeing back to Sicily in late 1958. This left Antonio Pollina, whom we discussed earlier, in the position of acting Boss in Ida's absence. Some sources do claim Ida did not flee, remaining in the United States. These, however, are sparse, to say the least, and it is widely held that Ida "settled in Fiumara and, within a couple of years, renounced the U.S. citizenship he acquired through naturalization" (Hunt, 2023). Ida would never return to the United States. Despite those in the Philly Mob calling him "the Boss who fled," Ida remained in Fiumara, spending his time hunting, with law enforcement's interest in him slowly fading to nothing. (Morello, 2005, p. 77). After the departure of Ida and the removal of Pollina by the Commission, eyes turned to who would next take the leadership of the Philly Mob. The Commission, who now had a say in the matter, had an idea of whom they wanted running the Philadelphia organization. That individual was Angelo Bruno.

# Chapter 3:
# 'The Gentle Don': Angelo Bruno

Up to this point in the exploration, we have witnessed the creation of the Philly Mob, its expansion from pockets of warring criminal factions to a unified Mafia family, and its inclusion amongst the big players of organized criminal entities in the United States. We have seen this burgeoning criminal organization led by five Bosses: Sabella, Avena, Dovi, Ida, and Pollina, each taking the reins of the Philly Mob in their own unique ways and all experiencing successes and failures. Now, we find ourselves on the precipice of Angelo Bruno's tenure as Boss of the Philly Mob. Portrayed on film in *Legend* and by actor Harvey Keitel in Martin Scorsese's *The Irishman*, Bruno, known as 'The Gentle Don,' saw out a 21-year reign over Philadelphia's criminal underworld; a reign so impactful that the family he ran became referred to as the Bruno crime family. In this chapter, we will explore this reign, discussing Bruno's style of leadership, his connections and relationships with other prominent mobsters, the events that led up to his eventual downfall, and just how brutal that downfall was.

## The Bruno Crime Family

Moving to the United States as a child, Sicilian-born Angelo Annaloro (Bruno later dropped that last name and began using his paternal grandmother's maiden name) was the son of a grocery store owner in Feltonville, Philadelphia, a store in which the young Bruno would "often [pick] up shifts" to help out his father (McKennett, 2019). He attended school briefly but dropped out after only a few years to open his own grocery store in Passyunk Square. Bruno's first of many arrests came in 1927 for reckless driving, and he "got involved in the Philadelphia Mob at a young age," his sponsor in the criminal organization taking the form of reputable criminal Michael Maggio. Bruno's falling in with the Philly Mob was the catalyst of his name change, reportedly doing so "as a homage to Philadelphia mobster 'Joe Bruno' Dovi" (McKennett, 2019). The rap sheet Bruno would accrue during the period before his ascension to Boss reads as familiar as any who were involved in organized crime, with arrests for illegal gambling, receiving stolen property, and firearms violations among the charges. Bruno also came to own numerous legitimate businesses, all of which did business outside of Philadelphia, such as an extermination company in New Jersey, an aluminum products company in Florida, and a share in the Plaza Hotel in Cuba, running them throughout his tenure as Boss of the Philly Mob. In context to his personal life, Bruno had married in 1931, having two children with his wife Assunta 'Sue' Bruno, with Bruno being "extremely dedicated to his family" (McKennett, 2019). Bruno, his wife, and children lived in South Philadelphia, and this was the residence from which Bruno "commanded the underworld" during his time as Boss (Hunt, 2023).

Technically, Bruno succeeded Joseph Ida as the Boss of the Philly Mob in 1959. Although Antonio Pollina had indeed taken over from Ida before this, his role was simply seen as 'interim' by all but Pollina himself. From the brief exploration of Pollina in the previous chapter, one can see that Pollina had a grudge against Bruno. After hearing of Pollina's plans to murder him, Bruno used his connections to the Commission to have Pollina deposed. Far from just being the Commission's top choice for the rank of Boss, they even gave him their blessing to assassinate Pollina. Bruno declined the latter and, by doing so, "displayed the mercy that characterized his reign by instead ordering Pollina into retirement" (Hunt, 2023). Under Bruno, the Philly Mob's power and influence grew exponentially, with Bruno expanding operations in Atlantic City, which had come to be known as Philly Mob turf. Law enforcement discovered in 1963 that Bruno and Phillip Testa had been making numerous trips to Atlantic City from Philadelphia, the fact being insinuated into both reinforcing the idea that Philly Mob operations were increasing rapidly in the area and that Bruno collaborated closely with Testa. Bruno also oversaw the Philly Mob's gambling syndicate, preferring more traditional Mafia activities such as loansharking, numbers games, and infiltrating legitimate businesses. Despite several arrests, Bruno avoided any substantial prison time, most likely due to his "connections with powerful politicians and power brokers" (McKennett, 2019). The longest prison time Bruno served came in 1970 for refusing to testify at a hearing regarding organized crime, for which he received nearly three years. Unlike his predecessors and fellow crime Bosses, "Bruno approached his criminal acts with the mindset of a businessman, which meant less gang violence and more profit" (McKennett, 2019). Bruno hoped that, by taking this path, he had "a chance to transform the mob into a more legitimate business" (McKennett, 2019).

Of course, one does not attain the nickname 'The Gentle Don' for nothing. Starting with the mercy shown to Pollina, Bruno preferred to seek peaceful solutions to issues and conflicts as opposed to violent ones. He had a "disdain for unnecessary violence" that came across explicitly in his style of leadership (McKennett, 2019). For example, he forbade his men from involving themselves in the sale of narcotics, fearing both the long prison sentences that came with them and the amount of attention from law enforcement that those activities would bring. That being said, violence was still the go-to tactic of the Philly Mob regarding anything outside of family issues. In the 1960s, the Philly Mob used violence and intimidation to great effect, allowing them to control various unions in the food and service industry and extort funds from a plethora of bars and restaurants. Still, Bruno's reign as Boss was predominantly one that "didn't rely on violence to get what [it] wanted," especially when considering the nature of the organization Bruno was leading and, because of this, "the Philadelphia rackets were never as profitable than when Angelo Bruno was in charge" (McKennett, 2019). This method of low violence and soft power was a far cry from the tactics of Bruno's predecessors and the violence that would subsequently come after Bruno's leadership ended.

# The Gambino Connection

Bruno was rather reputable in the eyes of those in powerful positions within the Five Families of New York and the Commission. Indeed, he had used these connections to depose his predecessor and was the ideal choice of the Commission to take over as Boss of the Philly Mob. Perhaps this push by the Commission of Bruno came from his distinct juxtaposition with the chaos of those before him. Indeed, the Commission was now responsible for keeping at least a relative peace between the Mafia families, and they needed a Boss that could simmer the frequent boiling pot that was the Philly Mob up until this point. His connection to the Commission aside, Bruno also had one specific connection that proved integral to his retaining power and respect: Carlo Gambino. At the time of Bruno's appointment as Boss, Gambino was not only the Boss of the Gambino crime family but also the head of the Commission. To solidify the point of Gambino's influence, after his son's marriage to Tommy Lucchese's (another powerful mobster and Boss of the Lucchese crime family) daughter in 1962, both Gambino and Lucchese controlled the Commission and most organized crime operating in New York City. That kind of power and influence was integral for someone like Bruno, who was attempting to change the very nature of the organization he was leading. It also helped that Gambino shared Bruno's distaste for the trafficking of narcotics, regardless of the profits it brought in. With that in mind, Gambino would become Bruno's closest ally in the underworld.

Using his powerful connections, a knack for business, and close association with Gambino, Bruno developed and maintained respect from the other Mafia Bosses in the United States. With this, he cemented his position as the Boss of the Philly Mob. Speaking of connections, Bruno also rubbed shoulders with the glitzy and the glamorous, being "quick to indulge in the more glamorous parts of his lifestyle" (McKennett, 2019). In an interview, Jean Bruno (the daughter of Angelo Bruno) described her father's meeting with American superstar Frank

Sinatra. When asked whether he had greeted Sinatra, Jean commented that Bruno replied as such: "No. He came up and said hello to me" (McKennett, 2019). Jean Bruno also revealed that she once saw her mother trying on expensive jewels that transpired to have once belonged to actress Marilyn Monroe. When questioned, she explained that Joe DiMaggio (star baseball player and ex-husband of Monroe's) had "been heartsick over [Monroe] and given the jewels to his close friend Angelo Bruno" (McKinnett, 2019). However, despite Bruno's Hollywood friends, powerful allies, relative immunity to law enforcement, and thriving criminal enterprises, the boiling pot he was charged with presiding over threatened to spill over.

## Pressure Begins to Build

Though the power and respect commanded by Bruno served him well over his 21-year reign, pressure began to build around the armor of his reputation, and cracks began to form. As mentioned previously, Bruno preferred the more 'traditional' criminal activities conducted by the Mafia and disliked the rampant trafficking of narcotics, going as far as to ban Philly Mob members from participating in such activities. This drew the ire of many of Bruno's subordinates, who could not understand why Bruno held such an archaic viewpoint, especially when a large sum of money could be made. In fact, some Philly Mob family members went as far as to set up and run narcotic trafficking operations under Bruno's nose, one member being Harry Riccobene, who would later play a part in the ensuing power struggle after Bruno's exit. This ire from the Philly Mob members were exacerbated drastically as it became common knowledge that Bruno was allowing the Gambino family to sell heroin on Philly Mob turf in exchange for a cut of the profits, with Philly Mob members angered by the fact that they were not benefitting from the profits of the drug sales happening in their territory, but other criminal families were. These "strict limitations on the drug trade in Philadelphia" enforced by Bruno seemed, at least to the rank-and-file of the Philly

Mob, to not apply to those who could line Bruno's pockets (McKennett, 2019).

It was not just the members of his own organization that began pushing against Bruno at this time. The newly burgeoning Philly Mob turf of Atlantic City, which was becoming increasingly profitable for Bruno's organization, was beginning to draw the attention of the major crime families. Bruno faced immense pressure from the Five Families of New York to allow them a cut of the rapidly lucrative market in Atlantic City. A market that expanded even further when, in 1976, gambling was legalized within Atlantic City, not only immensely increasing the flow of money into the Philly Mob's coffers but also "[making] the region more attractive to outside influences" (Hunt, 2023). However, the Five Families had a problem accessing the gambling enterprise. Due to long-standing Mafia rules, they could only enter into and operate within Philly Mob turf, in this case, Atlantic City, with the permission of the Philly Mob. Of course, this proved to be too much of a push for Bruno, who was unwilling to give such permissions.

As we can see, Bruno was facing pressure from all sides when the 1970s rattled forward into its later years, externally from the powerful Five Families of New York and internally from his rank-and-file members. Perhaps the final nail in the coffin of Bruno's reign came on October 15th, 1976, when Carlo Gambino died of a heart attack at his home in Massapequa, New York. While Gambino's death was not particularly unexpected, he was 74 years of age and had been suffering from heart disease. With his passing went Bruno's key ally in the underworld, triggering the bubbling pot under Bruno to spill over.

## Bruno's Murder

Antonio Caponigro had been watching Bruno's ailing popularity closely. A 'made man' of the Philly Mob since the 1950s, Caponigro was the son of a wealthy banana merchant, hence his nickname 'Tony Bananas.' He had risen up the ranks of the organization and, by the 1970s, was Bruno's *consigliere*. From this position, Caponigro saw the end of Bruno's tenure as Boss looming and decided to not only hurry it along but to give the Commission a perfect replacement: Caponigro himself. Caponigro knew that he could rely on the support of numerous Philly Mob members after Bruno's death in his move for the rank of Boss and began to rally those within the Philly Mob who wanted a cut of the narcotics trade that Bruno vehemently denied them. With this in place and sensing the pressure beginning to bring Bruno down, Caponigro met with the Boss of the Genovese crime family and member of the Commission, Frank Tieri. The murder of key figures within the United States Mafia, while not out of the question when considering the protection of Mafia interests, was not to be taken lightly, especially in Bruno's case as a sitting member of the Commission. In order to do so, Caponigro needed the authorization of the Commission, hence his meeting with Tieri. However, Tieri had his own motives in the deposition of Bruno. Caponigro had various profitable enterprises operating in Newark, New Jersey, where Tieri also ran his own operations. In an earlier challenge placed before the Commission to decide who retained control over the area, the Commission had sided with Caponigro in the territorial dispute, effectively ousting Tieri from operating in the area. So, when Caponigro approached Tieri regarding his scheme to kill Bruno and take control of the Philly Mob, Tieri began scheming of his own. Lying to Caponigro, Tieri told him that he would be able to vouch for him in the Commission and that his plan could go ahead with authorization. Caponigro put his plan into action, believing that his plan had been blessed and that his ascension to Boss was all but confirmed.

On March 21st, 1980, 69-year-old Bruno was sitting in his car not far from his house in South Philadelphia at an intersection, being driven by John Stanfa. Suddenly, a shotgun blast rang out, hitting Bruno on the back of the head. Bruno died instantly, while Stanfa was injured but ultimately survived. While "it is still unknown who exactly pulled the trigger," it is safe to say that the gunman was working on the orders of

Caponigro (McKennett, 2019). The particularly brutal point is that Bruno's body sat in that car long after he had died and in complete view of the public. Reportedly, "people lined up in the street to get a glimpse of the infamous mobster, still sitting upright in the passenger seat" (McKennett, 2019). Surprisingly, images of Bruno's corpse at the scene of his murder are readily available on the internet. Be warned; however, they are not for the faint of heart. With Bruno's death came rampant chaos within the Philly Mob, but before we get there, Caponigro's story has one final act.

As soon as the Commission learned of Bruno's death, Tieri's scheme came to fruition. Called immediately before the Commission, Caponigro assumed he would be named as the new Boss of the Philly Mob. Imagine his surprise when, at the meeting, the Commission stated that the assassination of Bruno had not even been considered, let alone authorized. Surprised by this revelation, Caponigro turned to Tieri, desperately looking for support; for Tieri to tell them that it was, in fact, he that had given the authorization. Tieri denied ever giving such a blessing, and the Commission ruled that Caponigro had murdered a Commission member without authorization or, in other words, handed Caponigro a death sentence. Just under a month later, Caponigro's body, along with the body of his co-conspirator and brother-in-law Alfred Salerno, was found beaten and naked in the trunk of a car parked in the Bronx. Two other co-conspirators, John Simone and Frank Sindone were also murdered for daring to go against the Commission. For all that knew him, "Angelo Bruno will always be considered 'The Gentle Don'," but the relative peace and stability of the Philly Mob under Bruno was shattered in all but a month. With the death of their Boss and *consigliere*, the Philly Mob devolved into chaos, creating a battleground where the next war for power would be fought.

Chapter 4:
# A Struggle for Power: The Second Philadelphia Mafia War

The destruction and turmoil caused by the death of Angelo Bruno in 1980 and the effect this had on the hierarchy and structure of the Philly Mob cannot be overstated. The conflict known as the Second Philadelphia Mafia War lasted from Bruno's death until the mid-1980s, a four-year conflict filled with blood, subterfuge, and aggression. From the information laid out up to this point, it would be reasonable to assume that the violence apparent in the Philly Mob had subsided, the chaos giving way to order as the organization settled into place amongst the crime families of the United States. This assumption, however, is far from the truth. The death of Bruno acted as a gateway that opened up the Philly Mob to all manner of mayhem and disorder and saw the rise of one of the most violent and infamous mob Bosses to ever rule over organized crime in the United States. In this chapter, we will explore the state of affairs left in the wake of Bruno's demise, the details of the Second Philadelphia Mafia War, the tenure of two new Bosses: one short-lived and the other just beginning, and the structure of the Philly Mob as it comes to the end of the conflict in 1984.

## Power Vacuum

With the loss of its Boss, *consigliere*, and some top *capos* (captains in the Mafia), the Philly Mob had a large space at the top of its hierarchy waiting to be filled. Quick to fill the gap themselves, the Commission accepted Bruno's underboss Philip Testa as the new Boss. Born in Philadelphia to Sicilian immigrants in 1924, Testa had been very close to Angelo Bruno, the two having met after living in the same area of South Philadelphia.

Early law enforcement files on Testa describe him as a 'common gambler' in that his income was dependent on his winnings when gambling. Following the interesting pattern of mobsters being named after their birth family businesses, Testa was also known as 'The Chicken Man,' a nickname "that sprang from the Testa family poultry market" (Hunt, 2023). The nickname also may have been in regard to his distinct appearance, with Testa being described, somewhat candidly, as "[having] a face that only a mother could love" (Long, 2020) due to a supposed bout of chicken pox at an early age leaving his face scarred. The striking appearance of Testa aside, the new Boss of the Philly Mob began his reign in 1980, appointing Peter Casella as his underboss and Nicodemo Scarfo as his *consigliere*.

Testa's reign would only last a single year, ending in such a brutal way as to rival the death of his predecessor. In 1981, Testa was killed when a remote-controlled nail bomb exploded under the porch of his house as he attempted to open the front door. This killing was immortalized in the Bruce Springsteen song *Atlantic City*, the opening line of which is, "Well, they blew up the Chicken Man in Philly last night" (Springsteen, 1982). The 'they' that Springsteen is referring to are Testa's underboss Casella and *capo* Frank Narducci, who orchestrated the murder in yet another attempt to seize control of the Philly Mob. Earlier in the year, Testa, Narducci, and others were indicted on federal racketeering charges. Law enforcement speculated that "Narducci and Peter Casella arranged the bombing to take control of the Philadelphia Crime Family" (Hunt, 2023). This was not how the aftermath of Testa's killing panned out. Nicodemo Scarfo, himself eyeing the position of Boss, had his suspicions on who was responsible for the bombing, going directly to his friend and *consigliere* of the Genovese crime family Louis Manna and naming Casella and Narducci as the conspirators. In a meeting called by the Genovese family with Casella and Scarfo, Casella caved, ratting out Narducci and admitting his own involvement in the plot to take control of the Philly Mob. Casella, while escaping death, was subsequently banished from the Mafia, and fled to Florida. Narducci was not as lucky. In a revenge killing, Narducci was gunned down less than a year later by

Salvatore Testa, son of murdered Boss Philip Testa, who was also a member of the Philly Mob and carved out a reputation for himself as a hitman, targeting those that had conspired to kill his father.

With all other opposers either dead or exiled, Scarfo had made himself the only viable candidate for the seat as Boss of the Philly Mob. He quickly gained the endorsement of the Commission, and by mid-1981, "his bloodthirsty reign had begun" (Patmore, 2022).

## Nicodemo Scarfo Takes Power

Nicodemo was born in 1929 to Philip and Catherine Scarfo, Italian immigrants who had settled in Brooklyn, New York. When Scarfo was 12 years old, he and his family moved to Philadelphia, where the future mobster would spend his formative years. Nicknamed 'Little Nicky' due to his small stature, Scarfo began an amateur boxing career, participating in fights all over Philadelphia and garnering a reputation for his aggressive temper in the ring. After failing to make it as a professional boxer, Scarfo was "formally inducted into [the Philly Mob] in 1954" during the reign of Joseph Ida (Patmore, 2022). His uncle Nicky Buck, a Philly Mob soldier, had acted as his mentor, with Scarfo "being schooled in the Mafia life and trained to kill by one of the family's feared hitmen" (Patmore, 2022). As one might have already guessed, Scarfo's aggressive temper and difficult behavior were not exclusive to the boxing ring. In one instance, he refused to marry the daughter of Giuseppe 'Joe the Boss' Rugnetta, who was Angelo Bruno's *consigliere* until 1977, which left Rugnetta embarrassed and disrespected, causing a brief rift in the family. Then, one fateful day in 1963, Scarfo entered the Oregon Diner in South Philadelphia. Whether this trip was for business or leisure is lost to history, but Scarfo did neither, "taking exception to someone sitting in his preferred booth" (Patmore, 2022). The person in question was a 24-year-old longshoreman who engaged Scarfo, presumably defending his right to be seated in the booth. What exactly was said during this heated debate is another unknown factor; what happened next, however, is not. Scarfo grabbed a butter knife and stabbed the longshoreman to death. In the same year, he pleaded guilty to manslaughter for the fatal attack, serving ten months behind bars. Scarfo also served time in the early 1970s with his Boss Angelo Bruno and Louis Manna, whom he later called upon to dispose of his rivals after Testa's death. Even from Scarfo's history before his tenure as Boss, it is clear why Scarfo's rule over the Philly Mob was seen as "marked by violence and betrayal," and it was only just beginning (Patmore, 2022).

After Scarfo's ten-month sentence was up, Boss Angelo Bruno sent him to Atlantic City, New Jersey. There is much to be said about Scarfo in the context of Atlantic City, details of which are included in the next chapter. Suffice it to say that, in this new area, Scarfo carved out a very successful living for himself, creating the platform from which he set in motion his ascension as Boss of the Philly Mob.

## Scarfo's Reshuffle

It is 1981, and Nicodemo 'Little Nicky' Scarfo has decimated all opposition and become Boss of the Philly Mob. Scarfo immediately appointed long-time friend and ally Salvatore Merlino as his underboss and Frank Monte as his *consigliere*. This was the beginning of a vast reshuffle in the hierarchy of the Philly Mob, with Scarfo appointing those he saw as loyal to him, or at least individuals he could easily control, and ousting those from powerful positions they had acquired under Scarfo's predecessors. Scarfo then proceeded to demote *capos* leftover from the reigns of Bruno and Testa, replacing them with his own, who included Phil Leonetti, Lawrence 'Yogi' Merlino, and Joseph 'Chickie' Ciancaglini. This reorganizing of the Philly Mob's hierarchy angered many members who, having enjoyed favorable positions under the leadership of Bruno and Testa, were less than pleased when they were, at best, looked over and, at worst, ousted when Scarfo took over.

Additionally, in order to further solidify his position, Scarfo allowed the families of the Commission to operate within Atlantic City (a chance they had been hungering for since the days of Angelo Bruno) in return for the Commission's continued support of Scarfo's legitimacy as Boss. Again, this drove the divide in the Philly Mob deeper, with members aggravated by Scarfo's allowance of New York gangsters to operate in Atlantic City. Scarfo spent almost two years of the Second Philadelphia Mafia War in prison on a gun possession charge. Not one to let a prison cell get in the way, Scarfo managed to run the Philly Mob in the same brutal fashion from his confinement. While locked up from 1982 to 1984 in the low-security Federal Correctional Institution, La Tuna in Texas, Scarfo was constantly flanked by two bodyguards. Referred to by Scarfo as his *'pistoleros'* (the Spanish word for gunfighters), these associates of the Mexican Mafia showed just how connected, powerful, and indeed dangerous Scarfo was, even when behind bars.

It is prevalent to note here that, while Scarfo was indeed Boss of the Philly Mob, this fact by no means meant that the landscape of the organization had begun to settle in any discernible way, with the Second Philadelphia Mafia War spilling over into the beginning of Scarfo's reign, not truly ending until 1984. In fact, it is arguable that the nature in which Scarfo had achieved leadership of the family, one of aggression, subterfuge, and violence, continued and even exacerbated the hostilities. Despite this divide in his organization, Scarfo managed to maintain control, albeit predominantly achieved through brutal crackdowns and bloody murders. There was, however, one final hurdle between Scarfo and his wish for a loyal and obedient Philly Mob, and that hurdle was about to make itself well and truly known.

## No Tribute

During Scarfo's prison sentence from 1982 to 1984, a Philly Mob faction would begin to rise against him. Harry Riccobene, who had started his criminal career as a soldier under Salvatore Sabella in 1927, was a veteran of the Philadelphia underworld. Seeing the relative peace and stability of Angelo Bruno's reign fall into chaos and disarray after his and Testa's murders and disliking Scarfo's greedy nature, Riccobene was most definitely opposed to Scarfo as Boss of the Philly Mob. The straw that broke the camel's back, so to speak, came when Scarfo demanded tribute from Riccobene, a cut of the profits in his loan-sharking and illegal gambling enterprises. While customary, this greatly angered Riccobene as Angelo Bruno had allegedly never asked for a consistent or unreasonable amount of his profits, and that was precisely what Scarfo was expecting. Riccobene, as one can most likely tell, was not particularly keen on Scarfo, "[making] no secret of his disrespect for the new Boss" (Hunt, 2023). Thinking Scarfo to be an unfit and illegitimate successor to the position of Boss, Riccobene consequently refused to pay tribute. This sparked the Riccobene War, a sub-conflict of the larger Second Philadelphia Mafia war, a conflict that would cost Riccobene not only dearly but also finally cement Scarfo as the undisputed leader of the Philly Mob.

Riccobene was quick to strike where he knew it would hurt. His faction wrestled Scarfo for family control of all operations in Atlantic City. Knowing the extreme importance of the area in context to the family's profits, and with Scarfo currently in a Texas prison, *consigliere* Frank Monte hastily retaliated, telling his crew that they were to strip Riccobene of all his operations and take them for themselves. Monte did not stop there, approaching Mario Riccobene, Harry's half-brother, and ordering Mario to turn on Harry by leading him into a trap. This scheme of Monte's backfired, with Mario telling Riccobene about the murder plot. This move by Monte sealed his fate, as Riccobene, enraged by Monte's scheme, decided to strike first. Riccobene and Mario, along with hitmen Joseph Pedulla and Victor DeLuca, sat in a parked van across from Monte's parked Cadillac, waiting to spot him. After some hours, Monte appeared and attempted to enter his car. Pedulla fired three shots, killing Monte. The gang of hitmen, perhaps fueled by the momentum of their first hit, later attempted to murder Salvatore Testa, who, since the death of his father, had become a respected *capo* and deadly hitman working under Scarfo. This second assassination attempt would be unsuccessful, with the group being arrested by law enforcement.

Then came the death throes of Riccobene's insurgency against Scarfo's family. With all four men in police custody, someone was bound to squeal. That person was Mario Riccobene, who agreed to become a federal witness, testifying against Riccobene at the trial. He did this seemingly out of fear for his family, as his son had committed suicide out of fear of being killed by Scarfo in retaliation for his father's part in the murder of Frank Monte. Riccobene attempted to defend himself, stating that he had no involvement in organized crime, that the rumors of death threats made against them by Scarfo were just that, and that he was the one who actually tried to convince Mario, DeLuca, and Pedulla away from violence. All of his pleas fell on deaf ears, however, and Riccobene was convicted of first-degree murder and handed a life sentence. With Riccobene's imprisonment came not only the end of the Riccobene War but also the end of the larger war that encompassed it: the Second Philadelphia Mafia War. Through the brutal use of violence, aggression, and subterfuge, Scarfo finally crushed all those that dared to oppose his legitimacy as the Boss of the Philly Mob. The mob Boss still had six years of leadership left to live, and he was only just getting started.

Chapter 5:
# The Gambler's Fallacy: Atlantic City

Imagine, if you will, a series of coin tosses. You flip once. Heads. You flip again. Heads. A third time. Heads. A fourth time. Heads. What will the next toss be? Heads or tails? Many will say that it is more likely to be tails as the coin has landed on heads four times previously. However, this would be incorrect. The probability of any single coin toss is half and half. It does not matter how many times it has landed on heads previously; the chance is always the same: 50%. The assumption that the previous result of a coin toss is causally linked to the probability of the subsequent toss is an example of the gambler's fallacy. This example is relevant here as a way of representing the nature of Atlantic City in the context of the Philly Mob. Having been a part of the organization's sphere of influence as early as the territorial expansions of Joseph 'Joe Bruno' Dovi in 1936, Atlantic City was somewhat of a confusion for the Philly Mob, going from modest township to desolate backwater to lucrative metropolis as fast as one tosses a coin. The area was the backdrop for various enterprises, rackets, and infamous mobsters, and every criminal family in the United States wanted a piece. In this chapter, we will explore the history of Atlantic City, its relation to the criminal activities of the Philly Mob, and the way in which Nicodemo Scarfo used it to develop his stranglehold on the Philly Mob and rise to the rank of Boss.

## Crime and Atlantic City

Nestled between islands and marshlands on the edge of New Jersey, looking out over the ocean, Atlantic City first adopted that name in 1853, when the idea came to develop it into a resort town. Due to its location, the area was noted as prime real estate as early as the 18th century, when the first hotel was built there. A building boom in the city came in the early 20th century, with hotels and businesses springing up across the landscape and down the famous boardwalk. Known for its casinos and beaches, Atlantic City is the inspiration for the United States version of *Monopoly*, the home of the Miss America pageant, and has attracted development from heavyweights such as Donald Trump. Criminal activity seeped into Atlantic City early in the 20th century, during the Prohibition era, which was enacted in 1919 and lasted until 1933. Considered by many to be Atlantic City's 'golden age,' alcohol flowed, and gambling took place in back rooms and basements of nightclubs and hotels, and the area came to be known as 'The World's Playground.' In subsequent decades, Atlantic City's fortunes entered a period of constant shifting, both economically and socially. Though still a popular tourist destination in the modern day, the area never saw a boom quite like that of the 1920s and, more prevalent to this exploration, its resurgence as a profitable enterprise in the late 1970s. Of course, wherever an economic boom is happening, the chance for lucrative business is also present. This attracted the burgeoning criminal organizations that were settling into the United States at the time, including the Philly Mob.

In the Prohibition-era environment, racketeer and political boss Enoch 'Lucky' Johnson rose to power, taking full advantage of the non-existent enforcement of Prohibition laws in Atlantic City, purportedly making annual kickbacks of $500,000 from illegal alcohol, gambling, and prostitution operations within the city. While not affiliated with the Philly Mob, Johnson was known to not involve himself in competing with other criminal organizations in matters of business or turf, preferring to take a cut of every operation running through the city instead. Johnson's real-life nature is a far cry from the fictionalized version of him seen in HBO's *Boardwalk Empire*, who murders his rivals and competes with mob Bosses for control of Atlantic City. The real Johnson simply facilitated other criminal organizations by running the political machine of Atlantic County that allowed the many crime families to operate within Atlantic City. That being said, his tendency to take a back seat in the running of criminal operations did not mean that Johnson was shy about being seen with known organized crime members. In May of 1929, Johnson hosted a conference for top organized crime figures in the United States. This meeting was the brainchild of Charles 'Lucky' Luciano, soon-to-be family Boss and orchestrator of the creation of the Commission two years later, and saw a slew of infamous gangsters descend upon Atlantic City. One particular guest of Johnson's was Al Capone, and the pair were snapped on a stroll together along Atlantic City's famous boardwalk.

Of course, the area of Atlantic City, despite being located a state over, had long been thought of as the turf of the Philly Mob. Dovi had expanded his family's operations into the area during the 1930s, and due to the city being in the Philadelphia Metro Area, the Philly Mob managed to retain control there. This stranglehold became tighter under Angelo Bruno, who fought off the advances of the Five Families of New York, who were attempting to cash in on the growing popularity of Atlantic City as a place for gambling activities and alcohol consumption. In fact, the pull of Atlantic City played a part in Bruno's murder, with mob Boss Frank Tieri falsely 'authorizing' Bruno's *consigliere* Antonio Caponigro to assassinate the Boss in order to eventually take over Caponigro's gambling enterprises and set himself up in Atlantic City. The Riccobene War, as part of the larger Second Philadelphia Mafia War, saw a rebellious faction of the Philly Mob attempt to wrestle control of operations in Atlantic City away from Nicodemo Scarfo, who, being incarcerated at the time, pushed back through his *consigliere* Frank Monte. Speaking of Scarfo, Atlantic City was also the backdrop in which he amassed his power and influence before making his play for the leadership of the Philly Mob, the details of which are covered later in this chapter. It is clear that, throughout the history of the Philly Mob up until this point, Atlantic City was both a lucrative beacon and a brutal battleground, ever shifting from one to the other.

# Fall, Then Rise

After the initial boom of the 1920s fizzled out, along with the Prohibition laws, Atlantic City entered the era of nightclubs. Many popular nightclubs kept the area in the public zeitgeist through to around the 1960s when Atlantic City really began to suffer. Plagued by poverty, crime, corruption, and economic decline, Atlantic City became a ghost of its former self. The reasons for this downfall are many. It would not be completely inaccurate to place the blame at the door of both technological and social advances. At this time, World War II was still fresh in living memory, and a cultural shift was taking place in the United States. The automobile had become more readily available, and air travel dropped in price, expanding people's horizons and giving the individual more autonomy to choose where to travel and for how long. Culturally, the fast-growing popularity of suburbia played its part in Atlantic City's decline. With more and more families settling into private homes in suburban areas, they had luxuries such as swimming pools and air conditioning units at home, largely diminishing their need to travel to resort towns during the hot summers. As one can imagine, this drastically affected the landscape of the city, not only economically but also physically. Many of the great hotels that paved the streets of Atlantic City, and lined the famous boardwalk, were struggling with high vacancy rates towards the end of the 1960s. These once sprawling hotels were fated with either being converted into apartments or demolished entirely. In 1964, the Democratic National Convention was held in the city, the convention that nominated Lyndon B. Johnson for president. While this move was seemingly an attempt to save the ailing city (governor of New Jersey Richard J. Hughes had a close friendship with the Democratic presidential candidate), it only served the decline of the area further, with press coverage of the event highlighting to the general public the dire state of Atlantic City: filled with crime, poverty, and desolate buildings.

The overall decline of Atlantic City spelled disaster for the Philly Mob, who had been consistently operating in the area since the 1930s. By the

1960s, the area was viewed as somewhat of a backwater, a desolate place for any member of the Philly Mob unlucky enough to be sent there. While there were operations that continued to run in and through Atlantic City, they were small fry compared to the enterprises of the family back in the city of Philadelphia. That is until Atlantic City experienced a second wind, and that second wind blew strong. In 1976, New Jersey voters passed a referendum that allowed for the first legal casino outside of Nevada to be opened in Atlantic City. This was done in an attempt to revitalize a city on its last legs, which worked to great effect. Gambling had never been particularly popular in the context of the law in the United States. Predominantly, gambling had been explicitly outlawed in all of its forms, with those who had a proclivity for the pastime being forced to partake in secret. This was until legal gambling was introduced in the state of Nevada in the 1930s, setting the foundations for Las Vegas, which has survived to this day. When legal gambling came to Atlantic City, so did everything else, and rapidly so. Construction on new casinos started immediately, with them springing into existence up and down the boardwalk. Promoters, taking inspiration from Las Vegas, began bringing big-name boxing matches to the city to attract visitors to the casinos. Boxer Mike Tyson had the majority of his 1980s fights in Atlantic City, helping to push Atlantic City nationwide as a gambling resort. In six short years since the introduction of legal gambling, Atlantic City went from an unwanted backwater to a gambling metropolis. As we already know, Atlantic City was Philly Mob territory, and this resurgence had dollar signs all over it. The problem was that they were not the only criminal organization that knew it. Organized crime had become synonymous with casinos since their introduction in Las Vegas, and its connection to gambling had come even earlier. Atlantic City represented a lucrative business opportunity, and the keys were firmly in the hands of the Philly Mob. Amidst this fall and the rise of Atlantic City was a key individual we have already mentioned, and he would use this area well and truly to his advantage.

# Scarfo's Stomping Ground

When Scarfo was released from prison in 1964, he "returned to the streets of South Philadelphia to unwelcome news" (Patmore, 2022). Bruno was extremely displeased with Scarfo. Brutally stabbing a longshoreman to death for no discernible reason was not a good look for the Philly Mob, especially under the leadership of 'The Gentle Don.' Bruno hated unnecessary violence, and Scarfo personified it, hence the friction between the two. As punishment, and perhaps to remove the unpredictable Scarfo from the main operations of the family, Bruno sent him to oversee the operations in Atlantic City. This was putting it nicely, as Atlantic City in the mid-1960s was not exactly a place where a burgeoning Mafia member could thrive. Scarfo had been banished for all intents and purposes and "may as well have landed on the Moon" (Patmore, 2022). Scarfo "scraped out a living with a bookmaking operation," living in the Italian area of Ducktown, Atlantic City. He was not alone, however, with his sister and mother living in the same apartment complex, along with Scarfo's young nephew and his future underboss Philip Leonetti. And this is where Scarfo stayed, away from the limelight of Philadelphia, where he could not cause the Philly Mob any more trouble. That was, however, until 1976.

When the introduction of legalized gambling hit Atlantic City, Scarfo made sure he would be catching the wave. Leonetti, who was in his early 20s at the time, recalled himself and his uncle Scarfo watching the announcement on television. During the announcement, New Jersey state governor Brendan Byrne had a provocative message for organized crime, exclaiming, "keep your filthy hands off our Atlantic City; keep the hell out of our state" (Patmore, 2022). As Leonetti puts it, after hearing Byrne's comment, Scarfo turned to Leonetti and said, "What's this guy talking about? Doesn't he know we're already here?" (Patmore, 2022). With this, the rise of Atlantic City as a gambling mecca would also see the rise of Nicodemo Scarfo as a powerhouse member of the Philly Mob, cementing his leadership of the organization. Together with his nephew

Leonetti, Scarfo set up a concrete company called 'Scarf Inc.,' of which Leonetti was president, and a company called 'Nat-Nat Inc.' which installed steel rods that reinforced concrete. "No new casino would be built without either" (Patmore, 2022). Considering the multitude of new casinos being built to take advantage of the new gambling legislation, these companies proved very lucrative for Scarfo. This fact was doubly true as Scarfo would employ harsh intimidation tactics to force companies to buy their materials from him. This was typical of Scarfo, who, while known for idolizing fellow mobster Al Capone, differed from him greatly in his style. Capone was known for his wit and charisma, while "Scarfo had neither," having "no sense of charisma; not even a hint of the old Mafia mystique" (Roberts, 2017). It is clear from the way Scarfo ran his enterprises, and indeed the way he ran the Philly Mob generally, that "Scarfo was a bully with a gun" (Roberts, 2017). Despite this rather unflattering character description, Scarfo's style worked wonders. *The New York Times* reported that, by 1987, Scarfo had made "$3.5 million through at least eight casino construction projects and other city infrastructure projects" (Patmore, 2022).

The construction business was not the only enterprise that Scarfo had a hand in. He employed more common mafia tactics in order to truly solidify his position as the dominant power in Atlantic City. He extorted money from the casinos he had helped build, controlling the local branch of the Bartenders and Hotel Workers Union through intimidation. With this, he could make sure that money kept flowing in the casinos by "[threatening] massively expensive labor disruptions" (Patmore, 2022). Perhaps unsurprisingly, intimidation also exploded into violence when, in 1978, Scarfo and Nicholas 'Nick the Blade' Virgilio murdered Judge Edwin Helfant "execution-style in a restaurant as he dined with his wife" (Roberts, 2017). Helfant was murdered after refusing to accept a $12,000 bribe to get Virgilio, who was facing murder charges at the time, a lighter sentence. While Virgilio carried out the murder, Scarfo acted as the getaway driver. Helfant's murder was a public execution, a message that showed what would happen if Nicodemo Scarfo did not get what he wanted. However, violence was not exclusive to not accepting bribes, as a contractor and frequent criminal associate of Scarfo's Vincent Falcone was killed on Scarfo's orders by Leonetti. His crime: making negative remarks about both Scarfo and his company. As Scarfo carved out an empire for himself in Atlantic City, the brutal conflict that would become the Second Philadelphia Mafia War was brewing. As we know, Scarfo was one side of that conflict, emerging victorious in 1984. With nobody standing in his way, his role as Boss of the Philly Mob secured by the Commission, and a host of lucrative enterprises in Atlantic City and beyond, Scarfo was one of the most powerful mob Bosses in the United States. But his unpredictability and hubris would catch up to him, and it would all come crashing down by the end of the decade.

Chapter 6:
# Ruthless and Paranoid: Nicodemo 'Little Nicky' Scarfo

By this point in the exploration, we have already been introduced to Nicodemo 'Little Nicky' Scarfo, his predisposition for violence, his casino empire in Atlantic City, and his victory against insurgencies within the Philly Mob when he took leadership of the organization. If we can believe anything so far, it is that Scarfo used brutal violence and shrewd business tactics to obtain his stranglehold of power and influence. However, it is infinitely harder to believe that this brutality not only continued but became much worse. George Anastasia, author and former journalist for *The Philadelphia Inquirer*, wrote this regarding Scarfo: "a greedy, ruthless despot whose family coat of arms could have been a pair of crossed .357 magnums mounted on a blood-red shield embossed with the words 'Kill or be Killed'" (Roberts, 2017). In this chapter, we will explore the Philly Mob during Scarfo's reign after he emerged victorious in 1984, his mental state during this time, and his eventual downfall, which saw even those closest to Scarfo turn against him out of fear.

## The Mob Under Scarfo

Scarfo wasted no time shaping the Philly Mob to be an organization fit for him to rule over, using the criminal family as a weapon to beat anyone who dared cross him mercilessly. His goal was to unify all organized crime in his territory, creating a well-oiled criminal empire to rule over. Soon after becoming Boss, in a move that proved his "management style to be grounded in greed," he imposed a 'street tax' on all criminal rackets in Philadelphia and South Jersey, "even [from] petty criminals" (Roberts,

2017). This weekly tax came as a shock to many as, while extorting cuts from other criminals was a regular Mafia racket, it was considered unusual in Philadelphia, and those working independently from the Mafia were expected to pay. This gave Scarfo a hand in all manner of criminal activities, from drug dealing and pimping to bookmaking and loansharking. The price for not paying was the ultimate one, and Scarfo made sure that his soldiers dealt it out publicly and harshly. John Calabrese, loan shark, drug dealer, and pawn shop owner, was murdered by *capo* Joseph Ciancaglini and three other Philly Mob enforcers for refusing to pay Scarfo's tax. As was Frankie 'Flowers' D'Alfonso, who was brutally beaten by Salvatore Testa and Joey Pungitore before being murdered in 1985. Scarfo also ramped up the Philly Mob's influence on the labor unions in Philadelphia, just as he had done in Atlantic City. Having had a hold over the unions since the days of Angelo Bruno, Scarfo gripped them even harder. The Philly Mob maintained degrees of influence over the local branches of numerous unions: the Roofers Union, the Iron Workers Union, the Labor Union, and the Teamsters Union, using this stranglehold to siphon funds from unions and extort businesses. This was an extremely efficient racket for the Philly Mob, as it was very little work in return for massive payouts and benefits.

Scarfo was also extremely eager to involve the family in the methamphetamine trade. While the family dabbled in the trafficking of cocaine and marijuana during this time, meth was a drug that had become very popular in the Philly Mob's territory. Popularity equaled money, so it was integral to Scarfo that his organization take control of the illicit trade. This takeover started simply enough, with the Philly Mob beginning to extort money from local meth dealers. The Philly Mob then began supplying phenylacetone, colloquially known as P2P and the key ingredient to the manufacturing of meth, furthering their control of the drug trade. This did present a benefit to some criminals who began borrowing money from Scarfo's organization to finance their meth operations and hence started to work with the Philly Mob instead of being extorted by it. With control of the supply of P2P, the Philly Mob could generally keep on top of the meth trade in their territory. However, it was when Chelsais Bouras, Greek-American gangster and Boss of the Philadelphia Greek Mob, attempted to cut in under Scarfo on the methamphetamine trade in Philadelphia that matters became more complicated. On top of this, he also refused to pay Scarfo's 'street tax' for operating on Philly Mob turf. Enraged by this blatant disregard for his power and reputation, the hot-headed Scarfo ordered Bouras to be publicly killed for all to see. He wanted Bouras's murder to be an example to all other local criminal organizations that the Philly Mob was top of the pile. He decided this despite the fact that the Philly Mob had a lucrative history of working closely with the Philadelphia Greek Mob and that a proportion of his own family members were, in fact, involved in Bouras's drug trafficking operation. Whether Scarfo was aware of this fact or not is of little consequence. The only thing that mattered to him was making it abundantly clear to all of the primacy of the Philly Mob in all criminal enterprises that operated in his territory. So, as Bouras was eating dinner with company, including his girlfriend and even one of Scarfo's own soldiers Raymond Martorano, a gunman appeared at the table and shot Bouras to death, killing Bouras's girlfriend in the process. One can imagine that the collateral damage of the hit was of no consequence to Scarfo, who only cared about the message it sent: he was Boss, and people would do well to respect it.

## The Mind of a Mafia Boss

There is a story about Nicodemo Scarfo that perfectly encapsulates his psyche, one of pure ruthlessness and aggression. Reportedly, "he [Scarfo] was once said to have exclaimed 'I love this. I love it' with joyous excitement while watching his soldiers tie up the body of an associate he's ordered killed for insulting him by underestimating his power" (Patmore, 2022). There is nothing better than this that describes the mob boss so wholly yet with brevity. Indeed, this unpredictable and volatile nature ultimately led to Scarfo being ousted from the seat at the top of the Philly Mob. However, before we get there, it is important that we catch a glimpse of the inner workings of Scarfo's mind. Nicholas 'The Crow' Caramandi, a member of the Philly Mob under Scarfo, became a government witness towards the end of Scarfo's reign after being caught by the Federal Bureau of Investigation (FBI). In a *Time Magazine* interview, he described, amongst many things, what it was like to know Scarfo. Caramandi explained that "if you were in good graces with him, he loves you and you love him. But you never knew from one day to the next. He'd turn on anybody, and he drew no lines when it came to killing" (Behar & Caramandi, 1991). It seems that even those closest to Scarfo were never fully sure as to his motives and next actions, with "even an unwitting sneer [provoking] him to take violent revenge" (Roberts, 2017).

Indeed, Caramandi's statement regarding Scarfo's psyche can be reinforced by his actions during the mid-to-late 1980s. During this time, Scarfo "ordered the murders of nearly 30 members of his own family" (Patmore, 2022). One of these members was Pasquale 'Pat the Cat' Spirito, who was only inducted into the Philly Mob for two years until Scarfo ordered his killing. Little is known about Spirito's early life. The son of Stephen and Rose Spirito, he hailed from the Italian community of Chambersburg in New Jersey. Introduced to the criminal underworld by Joseph Ciancaglini, Spirito passed himself off as both a plumber and hardware store owner to mask his criminal activities. When involved in loan sharking and bookmaking operations during his early criminal career, he became a close associate of Harry Riccobene and his half-brother Mario, earning his nickname 'The Cat' due to his abilities as a con artist, possessing an attractive charm and demeanor. Remaining an associate of the Philly Mob, Spirito got his chance to become a full-fledged member when he acted as the getaway driver in the shooting of John Calabrese, after which he was inducted as a 'made man' into the organization under Philip Testa, along with Francis Iannarella and Andrew DelGiorno. Despite his close connection to the Riccobene brothers, Spirito had switched sides during the Riccobene War, aligning himself with Scarfo. Due to this change of loyalty, Spirito was almost killed when he was fired upon while driving his Cadillac down the street, the gunman working for Harry Riccobene. This attempt on his life was also in retaliation for the brutal murder of Samuel 'Little Sammy' Tammburino, who was shot 16 times after leaving his parents' pharmacy in South Philadelphia by Charles Iannece and Francis Iannarella. After Scarfo took power, Spirito worked under him as a hitman and recruiter, taking on associates Caramandi, Charles Iannece, and Ralph Staino Jr. before presenting them to Scarfo as 'proposed members'. It is speculated that it was this fact that rubbed Scarfo up the wrong way regarding Spirito, with Philip Leonetti (Scarfo's nephew and late-reign underboss) later stating that Scarfo was furious at Spirito for suggesting who should be made *capos* and soldiers, feeling insulted that his underling was telling him how to run the organization. When Spirito later hesitated when Scarfo ordered him to kill Richard Riccobene, Harry Riccobene's brother, Scarfo snapped and ordered a hit on Spirito. Perhaps for a hint of irony or poetic justice, Scarfo chose Caramandi for the job, on which Caramandi said, "what was I gonna do? It was kill or be killed. There was no 'no'" (Behar & Caramandi, 1991). Caramandi went on to describe the brutal nature of killing those close to you, explaining, "Pat had bad vibes and knew what was coming. He had me in this booth in a luncheonette drinking coffee for four hours, making me tell him how much I loved him, and it's already set up to kill him the next night" (Behar & Caramandi, 1991).

Scarfo was beginning to become notorious for his ruthless nature and paranoid demeanor, constantly shifting his feelings about his closest associates, himself severely paranoid about dishonest and disloyal underlings. With any hint of perceived disrespect or insubordination came swift and brutal retribution from Scarfo, usually by close family members in a public setting. Caramandi states that "Scarfo was a cowboy. He didn't want a guy taken into a house and shot easily in the back of the head. He wanted it outside, in broad daylight, with a million people around. Restaurants, funeral homes, anywhere. Then it gets written up in the papers, and it puts fear in people. He loved that cowboy stuff" (Behar & Caramandi, 1991). With the number of murders associated with organized crime rising exponentially during his reign, it was clear that the Philly Mob under Scarfo was unsustainable. It would only be a matter of time before the organization Scarfo desperately held onto would turn against him. As Caramandi said, "he [Scarfo] was very, very paranoid. He betrayed himself" (Behar & Caramandi, 1991).

## Scarfo's Downfall

The fact that Scarfo was ordering the murders of his own loyal family members did not go unnoticed. However, it was the 1984 killing of Salvatore Testa that truly saw the grip Scarfo had on the Philly Mob begin to loosen. The son of former Boss Philip Testa, Salvatore Testa had proven himself "an extraordinarily efficient and loyal captain" under Scarfo (Patmore, 2022). Scarfo had allowed Testa to avenge his father's murder, with Testa personally seeing to the killing of many of the conspirators in his father's murder. However, the paranoid and obsessive Scarfo began to worry about the young hitman, believing him to be "rising too fast" and becoming popular enough within the Philly Mob that Scarfo thought he would eventually make a move against him. Salvatore Merlino, Scarfo's underboss, had a daughter that was engaged to be married to Testa. In 1984, the year of his murder, Testa broke off the engagement, angering Merlino. Caramandi, who eventually helped in the killing of Testa, stated this regarding the event: "Salvie [Testa] figured that by marrying the daughter of the underboss, he'd be right at the top. But she was a spoiled brat, and a couple of months before the wedding, he backed out. When Salvie backed out, he signed his own death warrant. It was a blow to the underboss. This was the ultimate insult. That night, it's time to leave, and [Merlino] grabs Salvie by the neck and kisses him on the lips. That was the kiss of death" (Behar & Caramandi, 1991). Using this as his reason, Scarfo jumped at the opportunity to get rid of Testa, permitting Merlino to murder him. On September 14th, 1984, Testa's body was found by law enforcement "bound by rope and wrapped in a blanket" at the side of a road in New Jersey (Patmore, 2022). While it is reasonable to assume that Scarfo was more than happy with the death of Salvatore Testa, it solidified his reputation to other members of the Philly Mob, and indeed all other criminal organizations in the United States, as a disloyal, paranoid, untrustworthy, and dangerous individual. Caramandi, while being directly involved in the killing, encapsulates the wider feeling of Philly Mob members on the death of Testa when he stated, "It was just awful. We killed him in a candy store. I really liked him. There was no reason for it" (Behar & Caramandi, 1991).

Even with his reputation rapidly decaying, Scarfo continued to crack down on his own organization. After underboss Merlino's drinking problem became too much of a liability, Scarfo demoted him to the rank of soldier and appointed Philip Leonetti to the position. However, even Leonetti was beginning to turn against his uncle, "being disgusted" at Scarfo's actions regarding Testa (Patmore, 2022). In 1985, Scarfo sent Caramandi, along with a few other associates, to extort $1 million from real estate developer Willard Rouse. Rouse immediately contacted the FBI, who began an operation to take down Scarfo once and for all. During this undercover operation, the FBI sent in agents under the guise of being Rouse's representatives. This operation ended with Caramandi, who was indicted for his part in the extortion, turning on Scarfo and testifying against the Philly Mob. This opened up the Philly Mob, making Scarfo vulnerable to law enforcement, snowballing between 1987 and 1989 as charge after charge was brought against him; three charges stuck: racketeering, conspiracy, and first-degree murder. One by one, "Scarfo's men started defecting to the government," with Tommy DelGiorno joining Caramandi in testifying to receive both shorter sentences and avoid retribution from the ruthless Scarfo (Patmore, 2022). Finally, the final nail in the coffin was hammered in when Philip Leonetti, who was facing a 45-year prison sentence and "wasn't going down for his uncle," agreed to testify against him (Patmore, 2022). All in all, 15 Philly Mob members received prison sentences ranging from 30 to 55 years, including Scarfo himself.

# Ruling Behind Bars

Scarfo received consecutive prison sentences of 14 years, 55 years, and life for his convictions. Although the life sentence was ultimately overturned (he was acquitted in a second trial for the murder charge), Scarfo became known as "the first Mafia Boss to be sentenced to death" (Roberts, 2017). Scarfo began his sentence in 1989 at the Atlanta State Penitentiary. During the trial, Scarfo's personal life also suffered. His youngest son, Mark Scarfo, at only 17 years of age, attempted suicide in 1988. Having been bullied relentlessly by peers and classmates about his father's criminal activities and becoming increasingly depressed by his father's possible imprisonment, Mark hanged himself in Scarfo's concrete company office in Atlantic City. While his mother did find him and paramedics were able to resuscitate him, Mark's brain had been deprived of oxygen for too long as he suffered a cardiac arrest. He fell into a coma, which he remained in until his death in 2014.

The convictions against the wider Philly Mob had devastating effects, with "Scarfo's actions [decimating] the Philadelphia family" (Patmore, 2022). As the 1980s came to an end, so did Scarfo's bloody reign, fueled by paranoia and violence. Law enforcement had managed to cut off the head of the Philly Mob, and much more, with 21 members incarcerated, 11 under indictment, and six turned government witnesses. In a report by the Pennsylvania Crime Commission, it was estimated that only 24 members of the Philly Mob were not facing charges and were freely operating. With so many of Scarfo's men serving long prison sentences and only a small amount of boots on the ground in regard to Philly Mob members, the Five Families, and the Commission acted quickly to avoid another power vacuum in the organization. John Stanfa was endorsed to take over the Philly Mob as Boss. From his cell in Atlanta, Georgia, Scarfo learned of his deposition as Boss and that Stanfa had replaced him. Although never truly shaking off his criminal ways (he was named in a companion indictment to the extortion of a Texas-based financial group as recently as 2011), Scarfo died of natural causes behind bars in

2017, never again to walk the streets he controlled, stained with blood and chaos.

Chapter 7:
# The War to End All Wars: John Stanfa and the Third Philadelphia Mafia War

Nicodemo Scarfo's nine-year reign had left the Philly Mob in ruin. With the majority of their members either in prison, awaiting sentencing, dead, or working with law enforcement, the prospects of the criminal family of Philadelphia were not looking bright. With considerable influence from the Genovese and Gambino crime families, the Commission was quick to appoint John Stanfa as the new Boss, hoping to avoid yet another war for control of Philadelphia. In somewhat of a self-fulfilling prophecy, a war is exactly what they got. Against the backdrop of a long war-torn territory, a new battle would take place for the coveted space at the top of the Philly Mob, and after the smoke had cleared, a new kind of Philly Mob would emerge. In this chapter, we will explore the appointment of John Stanfa, the rising of another insurgent faction within the Philly Mob, the details of the Third Philadelphia Mafia War, and the development of a new type of leadership entirely.

## The Appointment of Stanfa

John Stanfa was born in Sicily in 1940 and was brought up surrounded by Mafia affairs. His brothers had all become *mafioso*, being 'made men' in the Gambino crime family. Emigrating to the United States at 23 years old, he listed his occupation as a bricklayer. After arriving, he settled with his wife in New York City, where he was quickly introduced to the Gambino crime family by his brothers and brother-in-law. It was arranged by the leaders of the Gambino family that Stanfa would work for Angelo Bruno, then Boss of the Philly Mob. So, by the late 1960s, Stanfa found himself in Philadelphia under Bruno. It is not entirely clear how often Stanfa was tasked with chauffeuring Bruno around, but this definitely was his job on March 21st, 1980. If it was just a task handed to him randomly that day, then Stanfa was quite the unfortunate man, as this was the day that Bruno was assassinated. Bruno took a shotgun blast to the back of the head while sitting in the passenger seat of his car just outside his home. While Bruno was killed instantly, Stanfa was injured in the shooting. There is no hard evidence to suggest that Stanfa had a hand in the slaying of Bruno, but there is at least some circumstantial evidence. He had rolled the window of the car down, supposedly so Bruno could smoke. However, an open window would have also given the gunman a clear shot at Bruno.

Perhaps Stanfa was not unfortunate after all and was placed there as part of the killing. Regardless, if Stanfa was involved in the conspiracy to kill Bruno, it was his connection to the Gambino family that most likely saved him from retaliation, as conspirator Antonio Caponigro was himself murdered by the Commission for the same crime. Stanfa was then called to testify before a grand jury concerning Bruno's killing, disappearing shortly afterward, again with the help of his connections. In December of 1981, however, he was found in Baltimore, Maryland, working as a baker in a pizza shop. Unceremoniously dragged back to Philadelphia to face charges, Stanfa was accused of lying to the grand jury regarding his role in the slaying of Bruno after it was revealed that Stanfa had meetings with mobsters soon after the death. Charged with perjury (falsely affirming an oath to tell the truth), Stanfa was sentenced to eight years in prison, serving six of those years. Free to walk the streets of Philadelphia again in 1987, Stanfa was soon appointed as the new Boss of the Philly Mob after the chaotic reign of Nicodemo Scarfo ended in a large portion of serving family members ending up in prison in 1989/1990. However, history tends to repeat itself when those do not learn from it, and there were certain Philly Mob members that did not take kindly to Stanfa's appointment.

# A Divide in the Family

The repeated intrusion of the New York families into the business of the Philly Mob caused friction within its ranks. Many of the younger mobsters in the organization were Philadelphia-born and took displeasure in the appointment of Stanfa. While being of Italian descent was still a prerequisite for membership in the Philly Mob, the Mafia tradition of Italian-born leadership had waned as the organization had modernized. Hailing from Italy and settling in New York under the protection of the New York families, Stanfa was seen as not having worked his way up the Philly Mob hierarchy and not understanding the territory in the same way as the Philadelphia-born members did. One Philly Mob member had this exact opinion. Joseph 'Skinny Joey' Merlino was the son of disgraced former underboss Salvatore Merlino, born in Philadelphia in 1962. His birth family was rife with connections to the wider Philly Mob: son to Scarfo's underboss and brother to Maria Merlino, who was briefly engaged to Salvatore Testa before the hitman's breaking off of said engagement and eventual murder. He was also close friends with 'made men' the Ciancaglini brothers Michael and Joseph, whom he had met during his school years.

It could be said that Merlino was raised specifically for a life in the Philly Mob. He first butted heads with the law in 1982, when Merlino and Salvatore Scafidi beat and stabbed two restaurant patrons in Atlantic City, with Merlino being found guilty of aggravated assault and possession of a weapon for an unlawful purpose. Two years later, Merlino was banned by the New Jersey Casino Control Commission from entering any New Jersey casinos, the same sentence being leveled at his father later that year. Salvatore Merlino would then, in 1988, be sentenced to 45 years in prison as part of the broader indictment of Scarfo-era Philly Mob members. A year later, in 1989, Joseph Merlino would follow in his father's footsteps, but with an altogether different outcome.

In October of 1989, Nicky Jr., son of imprisoned Boss Nicodemo Scarfo and member of the Lucchese crime family, was shot in Bella Vista, Philadelphia. Hit eight times, but not in any vital organs, Nicky Jr. survived, and no one was ever charged with the attempted murder. That being said, the FBI and local law enforcement had a theory that placed Merlino as the orchestrator of the shooting. There was some bad blood between the Scarfos and Merlinos, and police informants have pointed to Merlino as the triggerman in the shooting. Apparently, Merlino "deliberately dropped the gun that night because he wanted to send a message" to Nicodemo Scarfo, who was incarcerated at the time (Anastasia, 2013). Scarfo was, as one can imagine, a big fan of gangster movies, one of his favorites being *The Godfather*. In a move identical to a scene in the movie, the gun was left at the restaurant. Merlino allegedly did so to show the elder Scarfo that he no longer had any power in Philadelphia. "Merlino had a score to settle that night," or at least, that is the leading theory of law enforcement (Anastasia, 2013). Merlino himself denied involvement in the shooting, claiming to have been under house arrest on the same night for an unrelated charge. Since his curfew was 7 p.m. each night, Merlino stated that he could not have been the shooter, "hardly a solid alibi, but his position nonetheless" (Anastasia, 2013). Years later, a rumor on the streets purported that, from prison, Scarfo had put a $500,000 bounty on Merlino's head in retribution for the attempted slaying. When asked by TV reporter Dave Schratwieser about the bounty, "Joey calmly looked into the camera in that classic Merlino-style and said, 'Give me that half million dollars and I'll shoot myself'" (Anastasia, 2013). Surprisingly enough, it was not this event that landed Merlino in prison. His incarceration was instead due to his involvement in an earlier crime where $352,000 was stolen from a Federal Armored Express Truck. This crime occurred in 1987, and in January of 1990, Merlino was convicted of planning the heist of the truck and subsequently sentenced to three years behind bars.

It was during this prison term that Merlino met Ralph Natale. A fellow Philadelphia-born mobster, Natale shared Merlino's feelings on John Stanfa. Both men felt that, due to Stanfa's connections to New York organized crime and the fact he had been in prison for the majority of Scarfo's reign in the 1980s, he was unfit to lead the Philly Mob. This is where the two insurgents hatched their plan to seize control of the organization from under Stanfa. There were other key conspirators in the plot: Michael Ciancaglini, Stephen Mazzone, George Borgesi, Gaetano Scafidi, and Martin Angelina. The rebellious Merlino faction would later be dubbed by the press as 'The Young Turks.' Stanfa, however, was aware of this divide in his organization. To appease Merlino's faction, Stanfa appointed Michael's older brother Joseph Ciancaglini as his underboss, hoping that this would bring Merlino and his supporters under the wider banner of Stanfa's Philly Mob and, by doing so, avoid yet another bloody internal conflict. However, this did very little to ease tensions. In 1992, another brutal civil war was fully in the swing for control of the family, known as the Third Philadelphia Mafia War.

The factions traded blows quickly and violently. Stanfa's loyal *capo* Felix Bocchino was murdered first, followed by a swift retaliation by Stanfa, who ordered the killing of Michael Ciancaglini, Merlino's right-hand man. The attempt on Ciancaglina's life failed, with Michael narrowly avoiding a hail of gunfire outside his home by diving inside and taking cover. The other Ciancaglini brother was not as fortunate. Having been appointed as Stanfa's underboss, young Joseph Ciancaglini found himself on the opposite side of the war to his brother. In 1983, Joseph was shot by three Merlino faction gunmen while managing his restaurant in South Philadelphia. While he did not die, he was left in a vegetative state by the brutal attack, the Merlino faction delivering a devastating blow to Stanfa with Joseph's incapacitation. Stanfa did not wait to strike back, sending gunmen to kill Merlino himself. In August of 1983, as Michael Ciancaglini and Merlino exited a social club, a car pulled up next to them, and the occupants opened fire. Merlino was shot four times and walked away, injured but alive. Michael was not lucky enough to cheat death a second time, being shot directly in the chest and dying. Not even a month later, a drive-by shooting was performed on Stanfa and his son. Driving on the Schuylkill Expressway, a van pulled up beside Stanfa's car and unleashed a hail of bullets. Stanfa escaped uninjured, but his son was shot in the jaw, only surviving as Stanfa's driver managed to lose the assailants and get them to a hospital. Stanfa's faction continued to attempt on Merlino's life, with Stanfa gunman Philip Colletti later testifying that he had planted numerous remote bombs under Merlino's car, none of which evidently had successfully gone off. In November of 1993, Merlino was sent back to prison, charged with violating his supervised release.

## Bugged and Jailed

Merlino's 1993 incarceration seemed like a win for Stanfa's faction. With the leader of 'The Young Turks' imprisoned, perhaps he could finally wrest control of the Philly Mob back and rule over a stable organization. Like many best-laid plans, however, this was not what happened next. While Merlino was supported by young mobsters he had known from childhood, Stanfa struggled to find the manpower from within the Philly Mob, as many were serving long prison sentences or killed after the Scarfo era. In an unusual move, Stanfa began recruiting criminals and hitmen who were not of Italian heritage, which broke a longstanding Mafia tradition, to maintain control of the organization and its territory and fight the ongoing war against Merlino's faction. With this being his main priority, "Stanfa brought in people who had no background in the mob but who were willing to break legs and pull a trigger" (Raab, 1995). Two of these individuals were the Veasey brothers: John and William. John Veasey would be the one who was intrinsic in dismantling Stanfa and his control over the Philly Mob. In 1994, Stanfa and 23 of his associates were indicted on multiple charges, from loan sharking and labor racketeering to murder. This came within seven years of the indictment of Scarfo and his associates, becoming the second federal indictment of the Philly Mob in so many years. Stanfa's indictment specifically holds the title of the largest prosecution of an organized crime group in Philadelphia history.

This prosecution was not something Stanfa could just shake off. The authorities had a key piece of evidence that deeply implemented Stanfa in all charges brought against him and his men. This evidence was two years of recordings taken of Stanfa as he explicitly discussed mafia business with mobsters in both his attorney's and doctor's office. Believing that attorney-client privilege and doctor-patient confidentiality would protect him from anything he said leaking, Stanfa would openly discuss business in these places, warts and all. What Stanfa did not know was that the FBI had obtained a warrant to bug both places after deducing that the offices were being used as meeting places for Philly Mob business.

Consequently, they had heard everything and had proof. With this overwhelming evidence stacked against them, Stanfa's men began to squeal. The Veasey brothers agreed to testify against Stanfa. On the day of Stanfa's trial in 1995, William Veasey, who was scheduled to testify against Stanfa, was murdered. A similar fate nearly befell his brother, but John Veasey escaped and gave the authorities information that secured Stanfa and 20 of his men's convictions. In July of 1996, Stanfa was sentenced to life imprisonment, which he still serves today at 82 years of age. With Stanfa imprisoned, along with many of his associates, it was time for Merlino, having been released from prison in 1994, to take his place as the leader of the Philly Mob. Merlino, however, decided to do things differently than those before him. Merlino named Ralph Natale, who was also out of prison, as the new Boss, positioning himself as Natale's underboss. While on the surface, it seems like a strange move to make, Merlino had a plan. Natale would serve as a distraction, someone for law enforcement to fixate on, while he pulled the strings from behind the scenes, away from prying eyes.

# 'Front Boss' Natale

A fellow Philadelphia-born mobster, Ralph Natale's father was an associate of the Philly Mob, running a numbers operation for the family. Natale himself was mentored by notable Philly Mob hitman Felix 'Skinny Razor' DeTullio, who "operated out of the Friendly Lounge where Natale tended the bar as a young man" (Burnstein, 2021). Under DeTullio's tutelage, Natale carved out a "formidable reputation as a racketeer and enforcer" for Angelo Bruno during the 1960s and 1970s, being Bruno's point man within the labor unions, specifically the Bartender's Union Local 170 (Burnstein, 2021). Former union leader Joseph McGreal demanded that Natale be removed from his leadership position, presumably suspicious of Natale's ties to the Philly Mob. McGreal was found dead in 1973, murdered, and Natale continued to help Bruno maintain control in the labor unions by "traveling around the country troubleshooting and greasing palms" (Burnstein, 2021). According to Natale, he became a 'made man' of the Philly Mob at a secret ceremony in Manhattan, attended by Bruno and Carlo Gambino, continuing to support Bruno as he expanded the organization's operations in Atlantic City through "a hostile takeover of bartenders, construction, and hotel and casino workers unions" (Burnstein, 2021). Natale also did not shy away from getting his hands dirty if requested, murdering conman George Feeney in 1970 on the orders of Bruno after Feeney began talking disrespectfully about Natale and Bruno.

Natale went to prison in 1979, just as Bruno started losing his grip on the Philly Mob. Convicted of arson and sentenced to 12 years, Natale was also convicted a year later for his part in the drug deal of 500,000 quaaludes and 10 kilograms of cocaine, for which his sentence was upgraded to 15 years. While in prison, he collided with Merlino, and the two began plotting their insurgency against Stanfa's Philly Mob. Although not released until 1994, Natale was still active during the Third Philadelphia Mafia War, "[commanding] a war that left a trail of bodies" (Burnstein, 2021). In 1990, he ordered a hit on two individuals:

bookmaker Louis 'Louie Irish' DeLuca and James 'Jimmy Brooms' DiAddorio, who were murdered within four months of each other. Released on parole in 1994, Natale found himself "as the don of the Bruno-Scarfo crime family" (Burnstein, 2021). He can be linked to two more murders in his tenure as Boss. One was in 1996 when Natale had North Jersey *capo* Joseph Sandano murdered for refusing to attend two separate meetings. The final one being Anthony Turra, who, before being able to come to trial for conspiring to kill Merlino, was found shot to death outside of his house. Natale's time as Boss of the Philly Mob was not what it seemed to be, with his underboss Merlino having far more power than his rank would have suggested. However, as much as he thought it, Merlino was not safe, as we will see that the influence of the law can be as far-reaching as that of crime.

# Chapter 8:
# The Politics of Crime: Ralph Natale and Joseph Merlino

From the Natale-Merlino era onward, we not only begin to see a shift in the way the Philly Mob as a criminal organization is run but also some key individuals whose presence is well and truly alive in the organization today. Natale's title of Boss was indeed only a title, the real power behind the Philly Mob being held by Merlino. This setup could have been the winning one for Merlino. However, his predisposition for flamboyance and love of media attention allowed the long arm of law enforcement to infiltrate the Philly Mob right at its highest levels. In this chapter, we will explore the events of the Natale-Merlino era, Merlino's personality as the "John Gotti of Passyunk Avenue," and the reasons for Natale's eventual betrayal of his own organization (Anastasia, 2013).

## The Puppet Boss

"Moving into a luxury condo along the Delaware River in New Jersey," one would imagine that, in the fall of 1994, Natale felt on top of the world (Burnstein, 2021). Having commanded and won a war for control of the Philly Mob, been given the title of Boss of the organization, and been released from prison, Natale set up his headquarters at the Garden State Park Raceway, "holding daily meetings at the restaurant on the building's top floor" (Burnstein, 2021). Unbeknownst to Natale, the FBI had the condo and restaurant bugged for "virtually his entire reign" (Burnstein, 2021). How much Natale knew of Merlino's power over him is unclear. Perhaps it did not matter, with Natale being perfectly content with his position. Or perhaps Natale saw it differently, thinking that the title of Boss would supersede all else and that he would always hold more power and influence than Merlino. Intriguing speculation aside, Natale did not just rest on his laurels during his four-year reign as Boss. While Merlino predominantly ran the organization, Natale positioned himself favorably within political circles. He managed to gain leverage with Milton Milan, mayor of Camden, New Jersey, "funneling the young politician with $50,000 in bribes" (Burnstein, 2021). He also began dabbling in the illicit drug trade and entered into an extra-marital affair with "one of Merlino's female contemporaries who was friends with his daughter" (Burnstein, 2021).

On the other hand, Merlino was not wasting any time in using his power. Merlino "[handled] collections and shakedowns in Philly," as well as overseeing the more general activities of the Philly Mob, that being gambling, loan sharking, extortion, and stolen goods rackets. He also spent this time developing beneficial relationships with other criminal organizations, such as the Pagans MC (of whom Merlino was good friends with the president Steve 'Gorilla' Mondevergene) and the Junior Black Mafia, of which Merlino was close with numerous members. The Pagans MC also acted as muscle for Merlino when underworld disputes broke out, further proving Merlino's intrinsic influence on the group. During the 1990s, Merlino would also avoid death numerous times, as hit after hit was attempted on him. In 1995, the leader of the Philadelphia drug gang, the tenth and Oregon Crew Louis Turra, was severely beaten and had his Rolex watch stolen by men working for Merlino for failing to pay the street tax on the drug money earned by the gang in Philly Mob territory. Merlino was doubly invested in teaching Turra's crew a lesson in respect, as they had also been warring with the Pagan MC motorcycle club. Turra was angered by the beating he received and wanted retribution. Turra's father, Anthony, organized a meeting at his house where he, Louis, and members of the 10th and Oregon Crew plotted to murder Merlino. This plot failed to come of anything, however, as father and son were both indicted in 1997 on many charges, including the conspiracy to kill Merlino. While awaiting trial in a New York prison, Louis Turra was found dead in his cell, allegedly having committed suicide by hanging himself in 1998.

It is heavily speculated that the Philly Mob (or indeed the wider Mafia) had a hand in Louis Turro's killing. What is more apparent is the death of the elder Turro that same year. In March, Anthony Turro (61 years of age and battling terminal cancer that bound him to a wheelchair) was mercilessly gunned down outside of his home by a gunman in a black ski mask. Anthony Turro was leaving his house that day to attend the federal courthouse, where a jury was deliberating on the charges against him and four others. In a statement from law enforcement, it was clear that they believed the shooting of Anthony Turro was a mob assassination. We know from the last chapter that Natale was linked to the elder Turro's murder, reportedly ordering the hit himself. Perhaps the Philly Mob was sending a grave message. Crossing them, or even thinking about crossing them, would be punishable by death.

## Merlino's Notoriety

While 'Front Boss' Natale provided a face to the Philly Mob as a distraction for law enforcement, Merlino's plan required him to work behind the scenes, holding power in the shadows by not drawing too much attention to himself. For anyone that knows even the smallest amount about Joseph Merlino, it will come as no surprise to find out that this is exactly the opposite of what Merlino did. Merlino gained a reputation as a flamboyant celebrity gangster, not unlike John Gotti or Al Capone, comparisons with which Merlino would most likely be very pleased. He was often seen at the fanciest locations, partying with a large entourage. The comparison to Gotti came from his candid and carefree demeanor in front of the camera. Indeed, unlike other mobsters, Merlino loved the media's attention. He would invite the press to philanthropic events he hosted, like "Christman parties for the homeless and [giving] away turkeys at Thanksgiving in the housing projects" (Anastasia, 2013). Being a "celebrity wise guy," Merlino was known for his general demeanor when interviewed, with his "dark eyes that can shoot daggers and the quick, staccato delivery when he's telling a story or asking a question" (Anastasia, 2013). Merlino loved the celebrity life, flaunting his power and influence whenever and wherever he got the chance. Still, like many of the fast-talking and wise-cracking mobsters throughout history, Merlino had a dark side. He never explicitly said it, but it was behind his eyes at all times, implicit in every conversation he had. He was powerful. He was dangerous. And he wanted people to know it.

Merlino was notorious for flashing cash and making huge bets with bookies. The problem was that Merlino refused to pay when he lost. This practice is known as guzzling, and Merlino single-handedly managed to pull this stunt at both mob-controlled and independent bookies. Merlino's continued flamboyant and reckless behavior began to grate on the wider criminal underworld. Through the arrogance and aggression of Merlino and his Philly Mob, many criminal gangs and individuals were unwilling to work for or cooperate with them. In June of 1998, after a short stint as Boss, "FBI agents arrested Natale at his condo on a parole violation" (Burnstein, 2021). Perhaps expecting his long-time friend and collaborator to give him aid, Natale did not panic. That is, until Merlino almost immediately took control of the Philly Mob, stopping all support for the imprisoned 'Boss,' "cutting him out of the loop" (Burnstein, 2021). This betrayal was devastating for Natale, who was now left facing charges with no support or contacts, having been "put on the shelf" by his own organization (Burnstein, 2021). However, if this betrayal was devastating, Natale's counter would serve to split the Philly Mob wide open, and Merlino was in his crosshairs.

## King Rat

Having been left high and dry by his former insurgent and ally, Natale was extremely incensed. As an instant reaction, he offered to secretly record conversations with Merlino. This, however, never materialized, and it was not until September of 1999 that Natale was able to gain any leverage in regard to his predicament. After being hit that year with an indictment in prison for "pushing crystal meth" (Natale had a hand in the sale of illicit drugs since his ascension as Boss), Natale "felt no particular loyalty to Merlino and spilled the beans on their entire operation" (Burnstein, 2021) in order to gain a more favorable sentence. With this decision, Natale became the first sitting Boss to become a government witness in American Mafia history. From 1999 to 2001, Merlino, his underboss Stephen Mazzone, his *consigliere* George Borgesi, Martin Angelina, John Ciancaglini, and a slew of other Merlino men were arrested and put on trial for various crimes: racketeering, illegal gambling, loan sharking, extortion, murder, and attempted murder. Reading like a comprehensive list of mafia organization activities, the proceeding trial was highly publicized. Originally, Merlino was only indicted for drug offenses (one count of conspiring to distribute more than five kilograms of cocaine and one count of unlawful use of a communications facility in relation to a drug trafficking offense), but this was later expanded to include the racketeering, murder, and attempted murder charges, one of which was for orchestrating the murder of Anthony Turro in 1998.

Just as in other eras of the Philly Mob, in the face of overwhelming charges and the prison sentences that came with them, many of Merlino's former associates and allies agreed to work with law enforcement, testifying against Merlino in order to receive lighter punishments themselves. Of course, there was Ralph Natale, but also many others peeled off from Merlino into the waiting hands of the authorities. Gaetano Scafidi struck a deal with police in 2000 while in prison because of fears that he would be killed by Merlino upon release. After being charged with two murders, Peter Caprio agreed to cooperate in the same year. Ron Previte, who was already working as an undercover informant for law enforcement by the time of the trial, also gave evidence. All of the turncoats testified that both Natale and Merlino had conspired and plotted to start a mob war with John Stanfa's faction in order to take control of the Philly Mob and that Merlino himself had participated in numerous criminal acts throughout the 1990s. Natale, during his testimony at Merlino's 2001 racketeering trial, also gave evidence as to the involvement of Merlino in numerous murders during the 1990s. However, "Merlino might have gotten the last laugh" as "Merlino allegedly kept Natale in the dark regarding details of certain murders carried out on his watch" (Burnstein, 2021). This withholding of information goes to show the shrewdness of Merlino's plan to install Natale as Boss while keeping the power for himself. Natale could not use information against him if he did not know it in the first place. "The jurors didn't buy everything the animated former mob Boss was selling on the stand." Consequently, Merlino was acquitted of all murder charges (Burnstein, 2021).

Merlino did not get off freely, however. When the jury returned a mixed verdict after hearing all testimony, Merlino was acquitted of all counts of murder: three counts of murder and two counts of attempted murder. He was, however, immediately found guilty of racketeering charges, including bookmaking, extortion, and receiving stolen property. Six of Merlino's associates were found guilty of various racketeering charges also. In December of 2001, a judge handed Merlino a sentence of 14 years. In response, Merlino clapped back, "Ain't bad. Better than the death penalty" (Press, 2001). Merlino was almost caught with a murder charge a month later when he was indicted again for the murder of Joseph Sodano, even though a jury found the murder charge 'not proven.' Later, in 2004, however, Merlino was acquitted of Sodano's murder. Taking his cooperation with law enforcement into account, Natale was given 13 years for drug dealing, racketeering, and bribery. He had admitted to committing eight murders and four attempted murders, so one could argue he got off with a light sentence. He started his prison time in 2005, being released six years later in May of 2011, where he was entered into witness protection. In his later life, Natale released a book entitled *Last Don Standing: The Secret Life of Mob Boss Ralph Natale* in 2017. In January 2022, at the age of 86, Natale passed away from natural causes.

# Chapter 9:
# To Flee a Sinking Ship: Rats

In the Mafia, loyalty will get you far. We only need to refer back to the opening quote of this book from Joseph Bonanno, who himself was the Boss of a crime family, to see that loyalty and reliability are desirable traits. To become a 'made man' in any criminal organization, those in power must trust you unconditionally, and if they trust you, they will protect you. That is the way that you survive and thrive in organized crime. That is, until it is not. After seeing Ralph Natale, who has the rather unceremonious title of "the mafia Boss who flipped," it seems pragmatic to now explore some of the multitudes of members and associates of the Philly Mob that broke the trust of the Philly Mob, turning on their family members predominantly in order to save themselves from the law. The fact of the matter is that, regardless of loyalty, crime is fickle. An individual's fortunes change rapidly and without warning. Besides, in a dog-eat-dog world that is an organized crime family, neither loyalty nor selfishness is guaranteed to keep you alive, and one must roll with the punches. In this chapter, we will explore some of the more prevalent and intriguing turncoats that have attempted to turn the Philly Mob over to the authorities throughout its history. From a corrupt police officer and a child mobster to a bulletproof rat and a psychopath's personal hitman, these accounts highlight the brutal, unforgiving world of organized crime and the lengths one must go to try and survive.

## From Cop to Bouncer to Soldier: Ron Previte

When Ron Previte returned to the United States after his time in the United States Air Force, he joined the Philadelphia Police Department. However, Previte was a bad cop. Depending on your definition of the word, this could mean many things. Suffice it to say that Previte became corrupt, saying that "he learned the most about how to be a criminal while working as a cop" (Anastasia, 2017). Born in 1943 in Philadelphia to Sicilian-American parents, Previte was raised in Hammonton, New Jersey. During his time in the Air Force, Previte served in Vietnam before returning to Philadelphia and joining law enforcement. During his time in the police force, Previte busied himself with activities that were arguably the opposite of what a cop should be doing, extorting traffic violators, shaking down restaurant owners, stripping impounded cars, stealing from crime scenes, and soliciting payoffs from bookies and mobsters (Roebuck, 2017). Moral implications aside, Previte was keeping himself busy. Unsurprisingly, he was forced to retire from the police force in 1979, saying, "I was asked to leave, but they never had enough to charge me with anything" (Anastasia, 2017). Two years later, Previte found himself working security at the Tropicana Casino & Resort in Atlantic City. Being "six-foot tall and sometimes 300 pounds, Previte was an imposing and intimidating figure," making him perfect for the job (Anastasia, 2017). One would also assume it helped immensely in Previte's criminal activities, which continued into his role at the casino. As an associate of the Philly Mob by this time, Previte stole chips and cash, stole all manner of items from the casino warehouse, robbed guests, and ran prostitutes and poker games out of unoccupied suites. As Previte puts it, he was "robbing the place blind" (Anastasia, 2017).

It was around this time that John Sheeran, a detective for the New Jersey State Police, began taking notice of Previte, who was fast becoming "a major and independent player in the underworld" (Anastasia, 2017). Sheeran started building a case against Previte, and after being arrested for theft in 1985, he agreed to begin working with law enforcement in exchange for the charges being dropped. Due to his work with the Philly Mob, the FBI also collared him to work as an informant, for which Previte was paid $750,000 from 1992 to 2002. The 1990s was when Previte got involved fully in the Philadelphia crime family when the mob had "replaced respect and loyalty with deceit and treachery, no longer a thing of honor," as Previte put it (Anastasia, 2017). By 1993, by using his abilities as a "shrewd and astute underworld entrepreneur," Previte had buried himself deep in the Philly Mob, earning big money, becoming a 'made man,' and even landing the role of Boss John Stanfa's personal driver. Previte fed information to the FBI and law enforcement throughout this time, wearing wires for the better part of two-and-a-half years. He later described his time wearing wires on a daily basis as "the most exciting time of his life" (Anastasia, 2017). With this information, law enforcement was able to indict and charge Stanfa and a large part of his crew. Though coincidental, this also saved the lives of many Natale-Merlino faction members, who were locked in the bloody internal conflict of the Third Philadelphia Mafia War at the time with Stanfa and his men.

After Stanfa's crew were indicted in 1994, Previte managed to align himself with the new regime of Natale and Merlino. While many of the faction's members, in hindsight, claim to "have been suspicious" of Previte, this would not be a problem for Previte, who alleviated any suspicions by bringing envelopes stuffed with cash to Natale and Merlino, provided to him by the FBI (Anastasia, 2017). Again, Previte fed information to authorities through the use of wires. These recordings (more than 400 hours' worth of conversations with Natale, Merlino, and others) were integral to the eventual downfall of the Natale-Merlino Philly Mob. "Faced with secretly recorded Previte conversations that placed him in the middle of FBI-monitored drug deals," Natale had little choice but to plead guilty and testify for the government (Anastasia, 2017). The recordings that included Merlino also helped to charge him with racketeering despite no murder charges sticking.

All in all, Previte's work as an informant for law enforcement helped to imprison over 50 mobsters, many of whom were members and associates of the Philly Mob. Refusing offers to join witness protection, Previte returned to live in Hammonton, explaining his rationale with "I like it here" (Anastasia, 2017). There he stayed until his death from a heart attack in 2017, aged 73. If there is anything to end the story of Ron

Previte on, it is this: "Ron Previte always lived life on his own terms" (Anastasia, 2017).

## Childhood Mobster: Phil 'Crazy Phil' Leonetti

Philip 'Crazy Phil' Leonetti should have had it great. While his father had abandoned him and his mother, she brought him up herself. The two of them moved to Ducktown, a predominantly Italian-American part of Atlantic City, from his birthplace in Philadelphia. And it was not just him and his mother; Leonetti had his uncle to watch over him in Ducktown, who was also a very prominent member of the Philly Mob. On paper, it seemed as though Leonetti would get a perfectly good start in life. But his uncle was Nicodemo Scarfo, who would go on to tear a hole in the Philly Mob's territory and fill it with blood, anger, and chaos on his way up to the top of the pile. Being connected by blood, Scarfo would bring his nephew Leonetti along for the ride. Appearing to be the direct opposite of his uncle Scarfo, Leonetti was calm, quiet, and reserved, both as a child and into adulthood. His nickname 'Crazy Phil' is somewhat of a red herring, given to him by a radio talk show host in 1973. Leonetti was not a fan of the name, and none of his Philly Mob associates referred to him as such.

Despite this picture of a reserved and laid-back person, Scarfo seemed to be adamant about inducting his nephew into the world of organized crime as early as he could. Leonetti alleged that when he was eight years old, Scarfo asked his mother whether he could take young Leonetti out for a drive. Of course, the young boy begged his mother to say yes. His uncle even said that he could sit up front with him. As they drove, "Scarfo told his nephew of the dead body in the trunk. He was a bad man, Scarfo explained, and sometimes you had to take care of men like this" (Patmore, 2022). Leonetti went on to explain that, after his uncle had brutally stabbed a man to death with an icepick in New Jersey for disrespecting him, he had used young Leonetti as a decoy as law enforcement were less likely to stop and search a car with a child in it. This fact was told to the young boy by Scarfo, and Leonetti said that it made him "[feel] special, like he was really helping his uncle" (Patmore, 2022). And, with that, "Leonetti had been sucked into his uncle's orbit. And for the next 25 years, he would rarely leave Scarfo's side" (Patmore, 2022).

Leonetti benefited from his uncle's position in the Philly Mob. Leonetti was president of 'Scarfo Inc.,' his uncle's concrete company. Also, by the early 1980s, and at around 30 years of age, Leonetti was a millionaire, controlling lucrative enterprises in loan sharking, racketeering, illegal gambling, extortion, and skimming money from the Atlantic City casinos. This reputation and wealth did come at a price, however. In 1979, Scarfo ordered Leonetti to kill Vincent Falcone, and he did so, shooting Falcone twice. This was far from the only murder Leonetti was involved in, later admitting to his part in 10 additional murders. A year later, Leonetti was officially inducted into the Philly Mob as a 'made man.'

As feelings of war began to bubble to the surface of the organization after the death of Philip Testa in 1981, his uncle Scarfo jumped at the chance to seize power, which he eventually did through aggressive and ruthless means. Later, in 1986, Leonetti would even be made Scarfo's underboss. However, Leonetti (along with many of Scarfo's other *capos* and high-ranking associates) had already begun to fear Scarfo's temper, paranoia, and unpredictability. After Scarfo's murder of his own loyal *capo* Salvatore Testa, Leonetti knew the situation was crumbling rapidly. "Testa's murder meant that nobody was safe, and Leonetti grew weary of his uncle's suffocating presence" (Patmore, 2022). Leonetti never got a break from Scarfo, as they lived in the same building, and Leonetti had become Scarfo's personal chauffeur, driving him everywhere he went. When Scarfo went to prison from 1982 to 1984, Leonetti described it as "the happiest period of [his] mob life" (Patmore, 2022). In 1988, when Leonetti was convicted of racketeering and 13 murders along with Scarfo and other Scarfo-era Philly Mob members, Leonetti decided that enough was enough. In what Scarfo saw as the ultimate betrayal, Leonetti (who was facing a 45-year sentence) "flipped and entered witness protection, becoming a very effective witness against Scarfo" (Patmore, 2022). This led to the conviction that put Nicodemo Scarfo away for the rest of his life. In a media interview in 1996, when asked how his uncle thinks of him, Leonettie replied, "I guess I never would be dead enough for him. If he could keep killing me, he would be a happy guy" (Patmore, 2022). For his part in the Scarfo-era Philly Mob's activities, Leonetti received 45 years. In 2013, after his release from prison, he released the book *Mafia Prince: Inside America's Most Violent Crime Family and the Bloody Fall of La Cosa Nostra*, which detailed his criminal life.

## Headshot Survivor: John Veasey

John Veasey's father was a violent alcoholic. When he was found dead in a hotel room in 1970, Veasey's mother, Sophia Maria Cuticchia, was left to support five children alone, of which John was the youngest. Veasey's eldest brother, William, became somewhat of a surrogate father to him, despite only being five years his senior. Unfortunately, Veasey's life did not get any easier from there, with Veasey saying, "we started fighting very young" (Cipriano, 2010). Fiercely protective of their mother, who was a bartender and continuously suffered from the unwanted advances of suitors, Veasey recalls when he was nine that, William, who was 14, "woke him up one night and handed him a stick, so the brothers could club into submission a boyfriend who had smacked their mother around" (Cipriano, 2010). The Veasey brothers were known to be tough street fighters, working out at the Goodfellas Gym at 16th and Passyunk in their hometown of Philadelphia. In the gym, John found that he had a knack for weightlifting, reportedly being able to power-lift 365 pounds. Despite his obvious physical talent, John was constantly bullied for the difficulties he faced as a student. "People told him he was stupid," and John seemingly believed them (Cipriano, 2010). Attempting to find other outlets, John fell into drugs, smoking marijuana at 11 and taking his first injection of meth at 14. It was around this time that John Veasey first fell onto the radar of law enforcement.

At 15, John was arrested after an incident at school. He had pulled a knife on one of his teachers and was charged with both aggravated assault and making terroristic threats. A year later, he was moved to St. Gabriel's Home for Boys after Cuticchia died of a heart attack at 41. Veasey's drug problem worsened, "turning to crime to support a cocaine habit that escalated to $600 a day" (Cipriano, 2010). William did attempt to support John at this time, albeit in the only way he knew how. William would beat up John if he caught him getting high and would also "beat up neighborhood drug dealers who sold to his kid brother" (Cipriano, 2010). In 1990, 24-year-old John Veasey was arrested for beating his wife's ex-husband, a beating so vicious that it ultimately led to the man's death. For whatever reason, the death was ruled as a drug overdose, and Veasey pleaded guilty to related charges, serving two years before being paroled in 1993. When Veasey was released from prison back into his home city Philadelphia, he would soon find himself "smack in the middle of the bloodiest mob war in the city's history" (CBS News, 2013). Boss of the Philly Mob John Stanfa was warring with an upstart faction of young mobsters led by Joseph 'Skinny Joey' Merlino, and between law enforcement and the ongoing conflict, Stanfa was running low on muscle. John Veasey, who now worked as a laborer at a concrete company, was a "rock-hard 200-pound slab of muscle" by this point and was all the muscle that Stanfa needed (Cipriano, 2010).

It was Stanfa's underboss Frank Martines that first approached Veasey about working for the Philly Mob. Martines offered Veasey $10,000 to kill Merlino, and he readily accepted the job. Martines told Veasey that he could have some time to think it over, but Veasey retorted, "take some time to get me a gun. And let's get it done" (CBS News, 2013). And, with that, John Veasey became a hitman for the Philly Mob. Stanfa, who was struggling to keep the family in order during the war with Merlino, was on a recruitment frenzy and, with Veasey, got "a guy who wasn't afraid to go out there and bust heads, and a guy who would go out and kill people if he was ordered to do so" (CBS News, 2013). Veasey and Phil Coletti were driving around the city, Coletti up front and Veasey in the back, on the hunt for Merlino. They found him on a street corner, chatting away with his right-hand man Michael Ciancaglini and a few others. Taking a closer look, Veasey spotted his brother William in the group, who was a childhood friend of Merlino's. Veasey told Coletti that they could not strike yet as his "brother would see [him]" (Cipriano, 2010). The pair drove around the block until only Merlino and Ciancaglini were left. As they strolled down the street, Veasey and Coletti pulled up beside them in their Ford Taurus. Unleashing a hail of bullets, the hitmen managed to kill Ciancaglini and wound Merlino.

After successfully killing Merlino's right-hand man and wounding the insurgency leader himself, Stanfa continued using Veasey as his muscle. Veasey also murdered popular bartender Frank Baldino as Stanfa felt that he was "[becoming] too friendly with the other side and wanted him dead" (CBS News, 2013). Veasey, although admitting that he liked Baldino, "shot him six times in the head" to make sure he was dead" (CBS News, 2013). Veasey also collected money for Stanfa, claiming that "he never once had to use brutal force on a shakedown" as "people paid because of his reputation" (Cipriano, 2010). Veasey proved this reputation when he was told by his brother William that he had overheard mobster (and cousin of underboss Martines) 'Joe Fudge' talking openly about killing Veasey. Inviting Fudge to his house, where Veasey was under house arrest and had to pick up a call from his parole officer, Veasey used a paddle-tipped power drill to rip out chunks of Fudge's hair as well as a baseball bat to strike at his knees. This example of Fudge was all being made while Veasey sat on the phone with his parole officer, the pre-recorded message "asking Veasey to repeat the names of American states in a precise order to prove it was John Veasey live on the phone" (Cipriano, 2010). Veasey's star was rising under Stanfa and the Philly Mob, but soon the tide would turn, and Veasey would find himself in the hands of law enforcement.

Still having not been paid his $10,000 for the hit on Merlino and Ciancaglini, Veasey began to question Stanfa as to why. The only money he was earning was a weekly payment of $300, which was less than his paycheck as a laborer. These complaints "did not sit well with Stanfa," however, and Stanfa then ordered a hit on Veasey himself (CBS News, 2013). When he learned that his little brother was in trouble, William, using his connection in the Philly Mob, warned Veasey and pleaded with him to work with the cops "to become a government informant: a rat" (CBS News, 2013). So, from 1994, at the behest of his brother, that is exactly what Veasey did. As part of his deal with law enforcement, Veasey agreed to wear a wire and collect evidence. He was not, however, wearing one on a fateful night in January of 1994, when Veasey was lured to an apartment in South Philadelphia by two men he trusted: Martines and *capo* Vincent 'Al Pajamas' Pagano. When he stepped into the apartment, everything was covered in plastic. "It's not normal to walk into a room with plastic," Veasey explained later, "but I did. I never thought anything" (CBS News, 2013). If he did not suspect anything, then he surely did when Martines and Pagano attacked him. Veasey was shot three times in the head and once in the chest by Martines. But John Veasey, as we have seen, was a fighter. Miraculously, Veasey survived the gunshots. When Martines then came at him with a knife, Veasey "wrestled the knife from [him], stabbed him, and ran from the building" (CBS News, 2013).

After surviving the assassination attempt, Veasey became a legend in the underworld. As George Anastasia explains it, "this is a guy who can't be killed now. And that enhances that whole reputation as a tough guy. John Veasey should have been dead that night, and he wasn't. I don't know [how it happened]. Maybe it's destiny. Maybe this was supposed to happen" (CBS News, 2013). Not that Veasey stayed in the Philadelphia criminal underworld after this. Entering the witness protection program in 1994, Veasey testified against Stanfa and his men, helping secure a conviction that put Stanfa away for life. His brother, William, was scheduled to do the same. He was, however, killed on the day of Stanfa's trial. Veasey was given ten years for his part in crimes committed during his work with the Philly Mob. Ever since his brother's murder, Veasey has been adamant that the Ciancaglini family is to blame. John Ciancaglini, along with others, was tried in 2001 for William's murder but was found not guilty. Veasey is now married to his wife of eight years, Norma, and became a car salesman, a job in which he seems to excel at, being nicknamed 'The Closer' due to his ability to "[sell three times as many cars as the average salesman" (Capriano, 2010). He lives under an alias after leaving the witness protection program, and "few in his new community are aware of his past" (CBS News, 2013). Far away from his old life as a Philly Mob hitman, Veasey claims that he has left organized crime behind him, stating, "like I say now, I'm not who I want to be. I'm not who I'm gonna be. But I'm definitely not the person that I used to be" (CBS News, 2013). However, many doubt Veasey's capacity for change, from crime reporters to residents of his old operating ground of South Philadelphia. Commenting on Veasey's newfound religious beliefs, George Anastasia ponders, "he's found God because it's expedient to find God, because he's somewhere in middle America, and it works to find God there. I don't think that if he's back on a street corner in South Philly, he's found God. He's looking to avenge what happened to his brother. He's looking to settle scores" (CBS News, 2013). Indeed, Veasey has made explicit threats against the Ciancaglini family, with John Ciancaglini's wife, Kathy, saying that Veasey has been intimidating her for years. "He believes that my husband has killed his brother," she states, "he threatens me, calls my husband a punk. He's the punk. He threatens women. It's what he does" (CBS News, 2013). It seems that only time will tell whether John Veasey has truly left his criminal past behind him or whether the pull of vengeance will prove too strong.

# Scarfo's Hitman: Nicholas 'Nicky Crow' Caramandi

A hitman and soldier during the reign of Nicodemo Scarfo, Nicholas 'Nicky Crow' Caramandi witnessed the bloody regime of Scarfo destabilize and eventually break the Philly Mob. From his position as Scarfo's top hitman, Caramandi watched as Scarfo, fueled by greed and paranoia, began systematically murdering his crime family members. Fearing his own head was soon to be on the chopping block, Caramandi, along with others in the Scarfo-era Philly Mob, such as Tommy DelGiorno and Scarfo's nephew and underboss Philip Leonetti, turned themselves over to law enforcement. While we have previously covered the reign of Scarfo in other chapters, it is prevalent here to briefly cover Caramandi's role in the wider activities of the Philly Mob at this time as well as his role in the eventual imprisonment of the ruthless crime Boss. Much of this information comes from a *Time Magazine* interview with Caramandi by American journalist Richard Behar, where Caramandi spoke at length about his time in the Philly Mob and his dealings with Nicodemo Scarfo.

Caramandi was recruited to the Philly Mob by Pasquale 'Pat the Cat' Spirito in the early 1980s, just as Scarfo took control of the organization. Spirito suggested that Caramandi, along with Charles Iannece and Ralph Staino Jr., become members of the Philly Mob, presenting them to Scarfo for approval. Unhappy with this (Scarfo was notoriously insecure and felt Spirito was questioning his authority), Scarfo ordered Spirito to be killed, and Caramandi was roped in to carry out the murder. As Caramandi explains, "We tried for months to kill him, and for a while, that's all we used to talk about. We used to get sick when we'd see him. We'd want to throw up" (Behar & Caramandi, 1991). Becoming suspicious, Spirito attempted to talk to Caramandi to put his mind at rest. Caramandi, rather coldly, reassured Spirito that everything was fine, leaving Spirito relieved. This conversation happened the day before

Spirito's murder. "We killed him in a car. Shot twice in the back of the head", said Caramandi, remembering the hit, going on to say, "I went round the corner to a bar and waited till it came on the TV news at 11. I said, 'Christ, they killed my best friend.' I was pretending like I was crying. This was my alibi. 50 people would have sworn I was there [in the bar] since 8 p.m." (Behar & Caramandi, 1991).

Caramandi also participated in the infamous murder of Salvatore Testa. This murder was the key to a large portion of Scarfo's inner circle turning on him out of fear. When asked about the murder of his friend Testa in the interview, Caramandi's eyes began to tear up. He explained, "You love him; you gotta do it. 'This thing' comes first. It comes before your mother, your father, your sister. It's the name of the game. If you're a gangster, you gotta be a gangster. You never know who you're gonna be told to kill in this business" (Behar & Caramandi, 1991). Caramandi's reaction to the assassination of Testa was similar to many members of the Scarfo-era Philly Mob, who felt that Scarfo had gone too far as Testa was a loyal and effective *capo*, his only perceived crime being that he was becoming too popular for Scarfo's liking. Giving further details about his role in the murder, Caramandi states, "I helped drag his body out, threw him on a road in Jersey, and left him in a ditch with a blanket wrapped around him. I seen his face when I turned the car around" (Behar & Caramandi, 1991). Suffice it to say, the murder affected Caramandi deeply, "I used to get nightmares over Salvie and would wake up in cold sweats screaming his name. This went on twice a week for three months" (Behar & Caramandi, 1991).

It was not just Scarfo's orders that bothered Caramandi and his fellow family members, however, as it seemed clear to them that Scarfo's psyche was unraveling right before their eyes. Describing Scarfo, Caramandi said, "He held grudges. If you didn't say hello to him 20 years ago, he never forgot. He used to say 'I'm like a turtle. I get there'" (Behar & Caramandi, 1991). Scarfo's soldiers and associates were terrified of him, and Scarfo made sure he knew what his underlings were thinking at all times. As Caramandi explains, "What Scarfo would do was take everyone to dinner and order double margheritas. Then he'd start talking about people, wants to see who chimes in, wants to see what they got to say. He'd make a guy drink and drink and talk and talk until there was no more talk left in him. I never talked because I knew this was a trap" (Behar & Caramandi, 1991). In 1985, Caramandi was sent by Scarfo to extort $1 million from real estate developer Willard Rouse. The FBI was informed immediately, and Caramandi was collared by law enforcement. As Caramandi puts it, "It wasn't my will to be a rat. I was arrested after the FBI had wired my construction partner for 18 months. I was in jail, and I believed I was gonna be killed there. I was scared to death. I was shaking. I blame Scarfo. He's the guy that wanted to kill me" (Behar & Caramandi, 1991).

In 1987, Caramandi pleaded guilty to murder, racketeering, and conspiring with a Philadelphia councilman to extort a real estate developer. In order to receive a more lenient sentence, and indeed to protect himself from Scarfo, Caramandi testified at 11 trials and helped with 52 convictions, including that of Nicodemo Scarfo, who was sentenced to life in prison. In regard to his feelings on his actions against the Philly Mob, Caramandi said, "all my life, I was a stand-up guy. I was loyal; I killed for the guy [Scarfo]; I brought him millions of dollars. There's no way I was ever gonna turn. It never even entered my mind. [But] you don't realize how precious a life is until you're in that position where you're gonna get killed, and you'll do anything to survive. I loved some of them guys. And I had to point the finger and bury them" (Behar & Caramandi, 1991). With this, Caramandi helped put away one of the most violent and ruthless mob bosses to ever operate in the United States Mafia, throwing the powerful Philly Mob into chaos.

## Chapter 10:
# The 'Modern' Philly Mob: Joseph Ligambi and the Return of Merlino

There is a saying that everything comes in three; a saying that, in context to the Philly Mob in the year 1999, rang exponentially true. In just under two decades, the organization had seen three massive law enforcement sting operations leading to the prosecutions of a large number of their members. It had been under the reign of three Bosses (if one counts the reign of 'Front Boss' Natale and underboss Merlino as one) who had destabilized the very structure of the Philly Mob. For another three, the third internal war within the organization, and the bloodiest yet, had also just ended, and the Philly Mob was once again left in a state of chaos. There is, however, one final act in the story, which is the history of the Philly Mob. After years under Bosses that brought the organization into the spotlight, along with all of its illicit activities and enterprises, leaving the Philly Mob vulnerable in the firing line of both law enforcement and the media, the time was now for a new Boss to enter the picture; a Boss that could douse the flames of a wrecked criminal family and move its operations back into the shadows. In this chapter, we will explore the reign of Joseph Ligambi, his ordering of a Philly Mob in disarray, the return of the flamboyant Merlino, and how the Philly Mob still holds sway in the modern age.

## Joseph Ligambi

Joseph Anthony 'Uncle Joe' Ligambi was born in 1939. One of four children of Italian immigrants, his father worked as a cab driver in Philadelphia, where Ligambi went to school before dropping out in his junior year to join the United States Air Force. It has become a pattern in this exploration for those individuals we cover to have early lives rife with criminality and violence, but in Ligambi's case, this is not his story. In fact, Ligambi's first entry into criminality did not materialize until he was 32, when he was arrested for smuggling cigarettes. He worked as a bartender in the 1970s at a bar that was frequented by mobsters, leading to his association with brothers Lawrence 'Yogi' Merlino and Salvatore Merlino, who would become a *capo* and underboss under Scarfo's Philly Mob. Salvatore Merlino was also the father of future Boss Joseph Merlino. This is where Ligambi's connection and standing with the Philly Mob began to develop, as Salvatore Merlino took Ligambi under his wing, with Ligambi becoming his protege. Salvatore Merlino was close with Nicodemo Scarfo, who would take control of the family in 1981.

Now an associate of the Philly Mob and being mentored by a notable member of high repute, Ligambi began helping run illegal bookmaking operations for Salvatore and made money in the process, earning a reputation for his skill in sports handicapping (especially for football). In 1981, Scarfo became Boss of the Philly Mob, and Salvatore was appointed as underboss, further strengthening Ligambi's connections to the upper echelon of the organization. Ligambi even became a 'made man' of the Philly Mob in 1986, at the age of 47. This connection to the top came with a price, however. In 1985, Scarfo ordered a hit on Frank 'Frankie Flowers' D'Alfonso, a Philly Mob associate who had already been beaten by Scarfo's men for not paying Scarfo's 'street tax.' When two family members, Thomas DelGiorno and Eugene Milano, became government informants, they testified in court that Ligambi and Philip Narducci were the gunmen and Frank Narducci was the driver in the murder. DelGiorno and Milano had been part of the planning of the murder, along with Salvatore Merlino and Francis 'Faffy' Iannarella, hence their turn as government informants. In 1987, Ligambi was arrested for his role in D'Alfonso's murder. In April of 1989, Ligambi, Salvatore Merlino, Nicodemo Scarfo, Francis Iannarella, and the Narducci brothers were convicted of the murder and all handed life sentences.

This could have ended Ligambi there and then, fated to fade away in prison for the rest of his life. However, in 1992, Ligambi's luck changed. A court panel overturned his murder conviction, citing misconduct from the prosecution and trial-court errors. In 1997, a retrial was finally held, and Ligambi was acquitted of the murder. When Ligambi was released from prison in 1997, the Philly Mob was in the Natale-Merlino era (Natale as the 'Front Boss' and Merlino as the underboss). Ligambi came back to yet another Philly Mob that he had connections with. Underboss and the one truly pulling the strings of the organization, Joseph Merlino was the son of Ligambi's former mentor Salvatore Merlino. Also, *consigliere* George Borgesi, who had conspired and fought on the side of Merlino during the Third Philadelphia Mafia War, was Ligambi's nephew. Still, Ligambi did not have much time to get used to this new hierarchy. In 1999, Merlino, Borgesi, and many other Merlino faction members were arrested, and it was Ligambi who was chosen to rule the Philly Mob as acting Boss while Merlino was in prison.

## A Period of Stability

Ligambi inherited a Philly Mob that needed decisive leadership, having been decimated by years of chaos, conflict, and shifting hierarchy. Indeed, "history indicates that the job of Philly Mob Boss leads to a jail cell or a coffin. Of the six mob Bosses who preceded Ligambi, two were brutally murdered, and the other four ended up serving long prison sentences" (Scarpo, 2014). Ligambi had in front of him a Philly Mob that was still wounded from the Third Philadelphia Mafia War, with the divide created during the conflict still feeling very present. Ligambi's family members were a mix of older generation mobsters from the Scarfo and Stanfa eras and younger generation mobsters who supported Merlino's 'Young Turks.' "The volatility for which the Philadelphia crime family was once well known can return as swiftly as the time it takes to pull a trigger," so whatever Ligambi was planning to do, it had to entice and appease both factions (Scarpo, 2014). Ligambi managed to do much more than just that, with him not only gaining respect, "ironically from both law enforcement and the Five Families," for stabilizing the Philly Mob but also unifying the organization's two factions, managing to "rivet these two enclaves together" to form a new efficient and strong Philly Mob (Scarpo, 2014).

When Ligambi took over as acting Boss, he cleaned up the mess before him. Firstly, he dismantled the idea of a Philly Mob Boss being explicit, loud, and in the limelight that had become a trend in previous years. Ligambi took a less aggressive approach to running the organization, rarely being mentioned in the media, and overseeing operations from the shadows. When picking his inner circle, Ligambi appointed long-time Philadelphia mobsters Joseph 'Mousie' Massimino, Gaeton Lucibello, and Anthony Staino and began to rebuild relationships that had been shattered by Joseph Merlino's flamboyance and arrogance. Ligambi repaired the Philly Mob's relations with bookmakers, whom Merlino would make huge bets with and refuse to pay them off, and a whole host of criminal organizations (both national and local), who were put off working with the Philly Mob due to Merlino's brash, aggressive, and arrogant nature. Also, during Ligambi's reign, a fair amount of 'made men' were released from prison, many of whom were young members swallowed up by the Philly Mob's unstable history and were leaving prison older and wiser. Ligambi welcomed them back and put them to work. In 2004, Ligambi made Anthony Staino his underboss, with Staino reportedly being Ligambi's closest and most trusted ally. Under Ligambi, the Philly Mob also muscled in on a new, more modern enterprise: video poker. The organization took control of several video poker gambling machine businesses within Philadelphia.

Ligambi was bringing the Philly Mob back into business, molding it into an efficient criminal machine that did not attract too much attention. That being said, one can only be so quiet when running criminal enterprises, and in 2007, law enforcement took notice. That year, 23 people, including four members of the Philly Mob, were charged with running an illegal sports betting operation out of a poker room at the

Borgata Casino in Atlantic City. Ran by the Philly Mob, this operation brought in $60 million in bets, of which the Philly Mob kept the majority of the profits. Most individuals charged pleaded guilty, receiving sentences ranging from probation to five years. Law enforcement did also catch up with Ligambi, although not quite as successfully as they might have hoped. In May 2011, the FBI indicted Ligambi and 14 other Philly Mob members and associates on racketeering charges relating to illegal gambling operations, video poker gambling machines, and loan sharking. Seven of those members indicted plead guilty to lesser charges, with one becoming a government witness. However, the authorities had a harder time getting a charge to stick with Ligambi. Two years later, in 2013, two of the charges were dismissed against him. In 2014, Ligambi and his nephew and co-defendant George Borgesi were acquitted and released. Just like that, Ligambi had "beaten the feds twice in a case that has landed 10 of his associates in jail" (Scarpo, 2014). By keeping relative peace, Ligambi managed to revive a dying Philly Mob. Still, "peace should not be mistaken for weakness," with there being three major murders unsolved that occurred during Ligambi's tenure: Ronnie Turci in 1999, Raymond 'Long John' Martorano in 2002, and John 'Johnny Gongs' Casosanta in 2004. There are only scraps of evidence in these murders, and the authorities have yet to piece together anything resembling a case against Ligambi for them. While quiet and peaceful, Ligambi was still a mob Boss and did what the job required.

## Merlino's Return

While Ligambi was rebuilding the Philly Mob, Merlino served his prison sentence at the Federal Correctional Institution of Terre Haute, Indiana. In March of 2011, after serving almost 12 years of his sentence, he was transferred to a halfway house in Florida, where he was to be on supervised release for three years. Just before his supervised release was to expire at the beginning of 2015, Merlino was handed a four-month sentence for violating the terms of the said supervised release by meeting with organized crime figures in Florida. In April of the same year, Merlino was released from the Federal Detention Center in Miami after his sentence was vacated, released ten days early after he won an appeal. In 2014, after being acquitted of racketeering charges, Ligambi stepped down as acting Boss due to the release of Merlino, who allegedly took his place as Boss of the Philly Mob, although Merlino himself denies this.

The 'organized crime figure' that Merlino had met during his parole in Florida was Nicholas 'Nicky Skins' Stefanelli, a soldier in the Gambino crime family. Stefanelli met with Merlino in 2011 to discuss numerous business ventures and projects, the nature and legality of which remain unclear. Merlino, who was "looking for a fresh start in Florida," was eager to hear him out (Anastasia, 2013). The start of the conversation went as expected, with Stefanelli focusing on the setting up of bars and restaurants, a venture he knew Merlino was interested in. However, Stefanelli had an altogether different agenda. He was wearing a wire and tasked with getting Merlino to talk about his involvement, past and present, with the Philly Mob. Stefanelli began to steer the conversation towards pending criminal cases of organized crime figures, including that of acting Boss Ligambi. Merlino made sure his answers were vague so as not to give anything that could be twisted against him, saying, "I said he was a nice guy, and I hoped he beats the case" (Anastasia, 2013). Stefanelli then asked about Nicky Jr., who was in federal prison awaiting trial on charges of extorting over $12 million from a mortgage company, with one of his co-conspirators being his father, Nicodemo Scarfo, 82 years of age and behind bars at the time. Again, Merlino spoke neutrally, recalling, "when he asked me about Scarfo, I said it was a shame what happened to that kid. I said his father was gonna get him 100 years, and I meant it" (Anastasia, 2013). A year later, Merlino learned of Stefanelli's wiring by authorities, stating, "the feds sent him down here to set me up. I told him I'm legitimate. I don't want nothing to do with any of that other stuff" (Anastasia, 2013). While Merlino continues to claim that he has nothing more to do with the Philly Mob and organized crime in general, the authorities seem to be having a hard time believing him. Indeed, they sent an informant to dig up dirt on him before he was even technically a free man. But Merlino proved in his conversation with Stefanelli "that he is savvy enough to know what to say and how to say it" (Anastasia, 2013).

In 2014, Merlino opened a restaurant in Boca Raton, Florida, named *Merlino's*, which has a menu filled with his mother's recipes. The establishment is owned by a group of investors as, due to his criminal record, Merlino is forbidden from owning an establishment that serves alcohol. As opposed to owning the restaurant, Merlino worked there officially as the head waiter until its closure in 2016. Regardless of Merlino's position on his involvement in criminal activities, trouble with law enforcement and other authorities manages to keep finding him. In 2016, the Pennsylvania Gaming Control Board banned Merlino from all casinos in Pennsylvania. In the same year, Merlino was arrested along with 45 others in a Racketeer Influenced and Corrupt Organizations (RICO) indictment. Detained at his home in Florida and brought to New York City for the trial, Merlino was charged with one count of racketeering, one count of fraud, and two counts of illegal gambling.

According to authorities, Merlino and the Genovese crime family had entered into illegal business arrangements. Merlino was also accused of participating in an insurance fraud scheme in Florida that involved doctors prescribing patients with unnecessary medication and billing their insurance companies. Later in the month of his arrest, Merlino was released on a $5 million bond. All other 45 individuals charged accepted plea deals, but not Merlino, who refused any plea deals and went to trial in January of 2018. After two weeks of testimony, a mistrial was declared after the jury could not come to a unanimous decision on any counts against Merlino. To obtain leverage and avoid a retrial, Merlino entered into a plea deal, agreeing to plead guilty to one minor charge in exchange for all other charges being dropped and a recommendation for a short sentence. In October of the same year, Merlino was sentenced to a maximum of two years in prison.

After a year, he was released early and served the rest of his sentence at a halfway house. A short time after, he was granted supervised release in South Florida. Merlino last appeared in the news in January 2023, when he was pictured with former United States President Donald Trump at a Trump-owned golf course. In recent times, Trump has faced criticism for certain individuals he has been photographed with (including white supremacist political commentator Nick Fuentes) and has supposedly introduced improved vetting protocols to combat the criticism. In the case of Merlino, the Trump campaign brushed off the photograph, stating, "President Trump takes countless photos with people. That does not mean he knows every single person he comes in contact with" (Dorn, 2023). His relationship with Merlino aside, the last time Trump and the Philly Mob were linked so openly was way back in the 1980s Scarfo era, when many Trump-owned hotels and casinos were built during the resurgence of Atlantic City. A tenuous link perhaps, and indeed one that may bear no deeper meaning. But an interesting observation nonetheless. So, whether Merlino is the current Boss of the Philly Mob, and indeed whether he is involved in any organized crime at all, is a matter for debate. But, as Merlino says himself, "I was found not guilty. What else can I say?" (Anastasia, 2013).

## The Philly Mob Today

Law enforcement, the FBI, and organized crime reporters all believe that, since Merlino's release from prison in 2011, he has continued to run the Philly Mob as Boss, with court documents from 2020 suggesting that, after stepping down as acting Boss, Joseph Ligambi now serves as Merlino's *consigliere*. The current underboss of the organization is Stephen Mazzone, who is presently in prison for illegal gambling, extortion, and loan sharking. Merlino, as we have seen, vehemently denies any involvement in the Philly Mob, citing his want to start an 'honest' life and his residence in Florida as proof of this, along with law enforcement's inability to prove any criminal activity. It is clear that if the Philly Mob is still actively operating (and it seems quite likely that they are), then they are doing it quietly, with many experts suggesting that they still maintain a stranglehold of power, influence, and stability, remaining to be one of the most active and powerful crime organizations in the United States. In 2016, it was reported that the Philly Mob had moved in on new business, with many members linked to the lucrative construction industry. In April 2018, four men made up of members and associates of the Philly Mob were arrested on drug trafficking charges in New Jersey, accused of distributing and selling large quantities of methamphetamine, heroin, fentanyl, and marijuana. The four accused pleaded guilty and received sentences between 5 and 15 years. In 2020, 15 members and associates of the Philly Mob were indicted on federal racketeering charges, amongst them being underboss Stephen Mazzone and *capo* Domenic Grande. The charges are somewhat classic for the organization: loan sharking, drug trafficking, and extortion.

# Conclusion

The approximately 104-year history of the Philly Mob is one filled with many things: power, greed, violence, subterfuge, and death, to name but a few. Through this exploration, you have been taken on a journey through the creation, maintenance, destruction, and rebuilding of one of the most intriguing, dramatic, and successful organized crime families to have ever existed. Seen the rise and fall of 12 Bosses who, through their wildly varying styles of leadership and personalities, held the Philly Mob high above its contemporaries in the criminal underworld and also drove it so deep into the ground that it almost could not get back out again. Lived through three brutal civil wars for control of the organization as factions warred in bloody battles for domination, leaving nothing but rubble and bodies in their wake. Felt the constant friction between the law and the underworld, infinitely dueling in a game of cat and mouse. And witnessed the dark intermingling of loyalty and betrayal and how one must know which choice will keep you alive the longest.

Ultimately, the individuals that find themselves operating under the banner of organized crime are doing so for a variety of reasons. They are there to make a living, to earn power and respect, to carve out a life for themselves, but perhaps most potently, they are there to find purpose, to be part of something greater than themselves, and to find a family. It is this human aspect of organized crime that we generally tend to forget, brushing over it in search of the more dramatic aspects that come with operating within an organized crime family.

The fictionalized versions of gangsters from movies and television, like the examples of which that are given at the beginning of this book, tend to lean on the side of glorification; they portray the gangster as the wisecracker, the underdog, even arguably the hero, and there is nothing inherently wrong with this. It is perfectly acceptable to root for the gangster, and no doubt should be cast on this fact. If one takes anything away from this exploration into the history of the Philly Mob, it perhaps could be that organized crime, while wholly within the public eye on the screen and in books in a fictional capacity, has been and still is a very real entity with very real power and very real consequences. Also, to keep in one's mind that those who make up the muscle of the Philly Mob are, despite anything else, human. As we have seen time and time again, organized crime can bounce back from devastating circumstances, and consequently, it is quite reasonable to assume that the Philly Mob, and the individuals that are associated with it, can and will do the same, holding influence and power over many aspects of our modern society as they have done throughout history.

That being said, it feels rather prevalent to end this how we started, with a quote that encapsulates the very nature of organized crime:

*Wherever there is opportunity, the Mafia will be there.* –Johnny Kelley

# References

Anastasia, G. (2013, April 12). *Skinny Joey Talks About Nicky Skins And Life Without The Mob*. Big Trial | Philadelphia Trial Blog. https://www.bigtrial.net/2013/04/merlino-talks-about-nicky-skins-and.html

Anastasia, G., & Sausser, L. (2017, August 29). *Ron Previte, the Former Mobster who Brought Down Three Crime Bosses, Dies at 73*. PhillyVoice. https://www.phillyvoice.com/ron-previte-former-mobster-who-brought-down-three-crime-bosses-dies-73/

AZ Quotes. (2023). *Johnny Kelly Quote*. A-Z Quotes. https://www.azquotes.com/quote/773987

Behar, R., & Caramandi, N. (1991, June 17). *A Crow Turns Stool Pigeon: Nicholas Caramandi*. Time Magazine. https://content.time.com/time/subscriber/article/0,33009,973168,00.html

Burnstein, S. M., Cassidy, K., McShane, L., & Pearson, D. (2021, February 18). *The Mafia Boss who Flipped*. The Mob Museum. https://themobmuseum.org/blog/the-mafia-boss-who-flipped/

CBS News. (2013, March 17). *Hit man: Has a Mobster Found Redemption?* https://www.cbsnews.com/news/hit-man-has-a-mobster-found-redemption/

Chase, D. (Executive Producer). (1999, January 10). *The Sopranos* [TV series]. HBO.

Cipriano, R. (2010, October 29). *John-John Veasey's Life After the Philly Mob*. Philadelphia Magazine. https://www.phillymag.com/news/2010/10/29/john-john-veasey-s-life-after-the-philly-mob/3/

Coppola, F. F. (Director). (1972, March 24). *The Godfather* [Film]. Paramount Pictures.

Dorn, S. (2023, January 23). *Trump Reportedly Pictured With Convicted Ex-Philly Mob Boss At Florida Golf Club*. Forbes. https://www.forbes.com/sites/saradorn/2023/01/23/trump-reportedly-pictured-with-convicted-ex-philly-mob-boss-at-florida-golf-club/

Dunn, M. (2021, August 18). *How The Apalachin Meeting Nearly Brought Down The Mafia*. All That's Interesting. https://allthatsinteresting.com/apalachin-meeting

Finkel, K. (2014, April 7). *Zanghi's Revenge: A Pivotal Mobster Moment – PhillyHistory Blog*. PhillyHistory Blog. https://blog.phillyhistory.org/index.php/2014/04/zanghis-revenge-a-pivotal-mobster-moment/

Helgeland, B. (Director). (2015, September 9). *Legend* [Film]. Studio Canal.

Hunt, T. (2021a). *Avena, John "Big Nose" (1893-1936)*. The American Mafia - Who Was Who. http://mob-who.blogspot.com/2011/04/avena-john-big-nose-1893-1936.html

Hunt, T. (2021). *Bruno, Joseph "Dovi" (1889-1946)*. The American Mafia - Who Was Who. http://mob-who.blogspot.com/2011/04/bruno-joseph-dovi-1889-1946.html

Hunt, T. P. (2023). *Philadelphia Crime Family Bosses*. American Mafia History. https://mafiahistory.us/maf-b-ph.html

Leonetti, P., & Graziano, C. (2014). *Mafia Prince: Inside America's Most Violent Crime Family and the Bloody Fall of La Cosa Nostra*. Running Press.

Long, B. (2020, February 14). *Remembering Philly and the Chicken Man*. The Northside Sun. http://northsidesun.com/news-columns-breaking-news/remembering-philly-and-chicken-man#sthash.NgIkeDQV.dpbs

Margaritoff, M. (2022, October 24). *He Led A Mafia Family For 35 Years, Then Wrote A Tell-All Book About It — And Somehow Lived To Tell The Tale.* All That's Interesting. https://allthatsinteresting.com/joe-bonanno

McKennett, H. (2019, November 4). *Angelo Bruno: The 'Docile Don' Who May Have Been Behind Hoffa's Death.* All That's Interesting. https://allthatsinteresting.com/angelo-bruno

Morello, C. A. (1999). *Before Bruno: 1880-1931* (Vol. 1). Celeste A. Morello.

Morello, C. A. (2005). *Before Bruno & How He Became Boss: The History of The Philadelphia Mafia Book Three: 1946-1959* (Vol. 3). Celeste A. Morello.

*Notable Name: Vito Genovese.* (2015). The Mob Museum. https://themobmuseum.org/notable_names/vito-genovese/

Patmore, N. (2022, August 4). *'A Greedy, Small-Minded, And Violent Terrorist': The Bloody Story Of 1980s Mob Boss Nicky Scarfo.* All That's Interesting. https://allthatsinteresting.com/nicky-scarfo

Pearson, D., & McShane, L. (2017). *Last Don Standing: The Secret Life of Mob Boss Ralph Natale.* St. Martin's Publishing Group.

Petepiece, A. (2018). *The Mafia Commission: A History of the Board of Directors of La Cosa Nostra.* Tellwell Talent.

Press, T. A. (2001, December 4). National Briefing | Mid-Atlantic: Pennsylvania: Mobster Gets 14 Years (Published 2001). *The New York Times.* https://www.nytimes.com/2001/12/04/us/national-briefing-mid-atlantic-pennsylvania-mobster-gets-14-years.html

Raab, S. (1995, October 6). Brother of Mob Turncoat Is Gunned Down. *The New York Times.*

https://www.nytimes.com/1995/10/06/us/brother-of-mob-turncoat-is-gunned-down.html

Roberts, S. (2017, January 17). Nicky Scarfo, Mob Boss Who Plundered Atlantic City in the '80s, Dies at 87 (Published 2017). *The New York Times.* https://www.nytimes.com/2017/01/17/nyregion/nicky-scarfo-mob-boss-who-plundered-atlantic-city-in-the-80s-dies-at-87.html

Roebuck, J. (2017, August 29). *Ron Previte, wiseguy informant who brought down Philly mob bosses, dead at 73.* Https://Www.inquirer.com. https://www.inquirer.com/philly/obituaries/ron-previte-dies-informant-mob-bosses-philly-20170829.html

Scarpo, E. (17, July 2014). *If Uncle Joe Retires What Happens in Philadelphia?* Cosa Nostra News. https://www.cosanostranews.com/2014/03/philly-mob-boss-uncle-joe-says-hes-done.html

Scorsese, M. (Director). (2019, November 1). *The Irishman* [Film]. Netflix.

Springsteen, B. (1982). *Atlantic City.* YouTube. https://www.youtube.com/watch?v=M3eu1gW-bQ8

Winter, T. (Executive Producer). (2010, September 19). *Boardwalk Empire* [TV series]. HBO.

www.ingramcontent.com/pod-product-compliance
Lightning Source LLC
Chambersburg PA
CBHW071403080526
44587CB00017B/3166